Glanville examines Exodus's call to be [illegible] communities" that restore neighbor[illegible] Family explores biblical leadership models that empower the marginalized. Readers will discover how God's holiness includes social justice and community-building. Glanville's passion for discipleship and neighborhood investment shines through on every page. This study provides excellent resources for churches to impact their neighborhoods for God's kingdom.

**LYNN COHICK**

Provost,

Northern Seminary

Forget about Charlton Heston. Mark Glanville shows how Exodus is about more than just Israel's escape from Egypt. It is a radical narrative about the creation of a completely different kind of society, declaring their allegiance to a whole new kind of King. Mark's excellent analysis of the biblical text will help shape the missional imagination of your church and equip you to live as a sign to God's magnificent reign.

**MICHAEL FROST**

Founding Director of the Tinsley Institute,

Morling College

Mark Glanville brings together everything you want in a biblical interpreter: he is scholarly, passionate, churchly, justice-hungry, wise and kind, at home equally in the classroom, the pulpit, and the streets. This book made Exodus sing for me again.

**JASON BYASSEE**

Butler Chair in Homiletics and Biblical Interpretation,

Vancouver School of Theology

It is always refreshing to look at a familiar biblical book through different lenses. Mark Glanville helps us enter creatively into the foundational epic of Israel's emergence out of dehumanising slavery into a community of covenant kinship—the family of God—with all the blessings and responsibilities of that identity. And since their story is our story, it is a book with powerful lessons for us who claim the same identity in the Messiah Jesus, and thus inherit the same missional challenge.

**CHRISTOPHER J. H. WRIGHT**
author of *Exodus: The Story of God Bible Commentary*

# FREED TO BE GOD'S FAMILY

## THE BOOK OF EXODUS

**Other titles in the Transformative Word series:**

# FREED TO BE GOD'S FAMILY

## THE BOOK OF EXODUS

### TRANSFORMATIVE WORD

MARK R. GLANVILLE

Series Editors
Craig G. Bartholomew &
David J. H. Beldmann

LEXHAM PRESS

*Freed to Be God's Family: The Book of Exodus*
Transformative Word

Copyright 2021 Mark R. Glanville

Lexham Press, 1313 Commercial St., Bellingham, WA 98225
LexhamPress.com

All rights reserved. You may use brief quotations from this resource in presentations, articles, and books. For all other uses, please write Lexham Press for permission. Email us at permissions@lexhampress.com.

Unless otherwise noted, Scripture quotations are from the from the New Revised Standard Version Bible, copyright © 1989, National Council of the Churches of Christ in the United States of America. Used by permission. All rights reserved.

Print ISBN 9781683594468
Digital ISBN 9781683594475
Library of Congress Control Number 2020946392

Series Editors: Craig G. Bartholomew and David Beldman
Lexham Editorial: David Bomar, Abigail Stocker, Elliot Ritzema, Kelsey Matthews
Cover Design: Kristen Cork
Typesetting: Fanny Palacios

*To the leaders at*
*Tregear Presbyterian Church, NSW Australia,*
*who first called me and ordained me as a pastor (2007),*
*and who then partnered shoulder to shoulder with me*
*in the tender work of the gospel in that particular place,*
*enduring patiently my passion and my mistakes.*
*Russell and Steph Baker, Ash and Des Davies, Dan and*
*Ali OpdeVeigh, David, George, and Emma Newmarch,*
*Di Scott, John Grant, Sally and Ray Davis, Bob and Joan*
*Blundell, Andrew and Amanda Malin, and others.*

*"I thank my God in all my remembrance of you"*
*—Philippians 1:3*

# TABLE OF CONTENTS

# INTRODUCTION

The book of Exodus is all about community. It is the real story of a society that was being reshaped as "family," under the lordship of Yahweh. At the opening of the book of Exodus, the Israelites were enslaved brick-workers in Egypt—before Yahweh intervened. In Egypt, human relationships were deeply fractured. The beating of a Hebrew slave and the destruction of male babies had become permanent symbols of the atrocity of slavery (Exod 1:15–22; 2:11–15). Yahweh emancipated Israel from slavery in Egypt and brought the nation to Mount Sinai so that they might be established in covenant relationship with God. God's laws shaped Israel to operate the way that God had always intended for communities to operate: in love, as kindred. The book of Exodus is all about the formation of this renewed community that lives together before the face of God. It shows us the joy, the freshness, the hope, and the imagination that a community can experience when it is transformed by the love of God.

While this book is the ancient story of an ancient community that encounters the love of God, it also contains an implicit invitation to Christ-followers today: to consider how Christ's word and Christ's presence may be nourishing our communities and our relationships in the direction of family. A thread weaving through the biblical story, one overtone within the heartbeat of Scripture, is Christ's renewing us as sisters and brothers, by God's gracious presence. To be sure, this dynamic of community is not the only theme in Exodus. However, God's reshaping of community is central to this book, and this is the lens through which we will view Exodus in our journey together. As you read through this ancient story, consider: Is there an invitation for your own worshiping community in the book of Exodus? What fresh ideas and imaginings is the Holy Spirit stirring in you and in your community as you read?

The call to community in the book of Exodus has very practical implications. To connect our own lives with Israel's journey from Egypt to Sinai, let me share with you a project that our worshiping community in Vancouver, British Columbia, is embarking on. (I was pastoring here at the time of writing, before stepping aside to teach at Regent College.) During the time of writing this book, our church has taken fresh steps toward community. We have, at long last, broken ground and begun the construction process for a housing project. We are transforming our church car park into a four-story affordable housing complex with twenty-six self-contained units and also tons of community space and plots for communal gardening. We call it the "Co:Here" building. While the rocketing cost of housing in Vancouver is splintering human relationships and also our relationship with "place," "Co:Here is founded on the conviction that people are made for community," so the blurb reads. Vulnerable people who are already connected within our community, many of whom have literally lived on the street, will live and grow old with people who have been lucky enough to have easier lives. As residents live together for the long haul, everyone will be invited into a process of mutual transformation. The Co:Here project illustrates a central theme in the book of Exodus: God's desire to shape society to live together in love as family.

## The Biblical Drama until This Point

It is helpful to narrate the biblical drama up until the beginning of the book of Exodus. God is the primary actor in the biblical drama. In the beginning, God created a good world with care and delight. However, God's good creation was soon corrupted by human rebellion. This is often referred to as the "fall" of humanity (Gen 3). Human relationships crumble as a consequence of human rebellion against God. Indeed, in the very next chapter (Gen 4) we encounter fratricide: brother kills brother. Every aspect of God's good creation begins to crumble, polluted as it is by sin's curse. In loving commitment to the creation, God set off on a long road of restoring the world to the joy and flourishing for which it was intended.

God called a people group, Abraham's family, promising to bless these people, to give them a land to flourish in, and then to bless every other people group in the world through them (Gen 12:1-3). The story of the call of Abraham follows the table of seventy nations, a list that is symbolic of every nation on the earth (Gen 10). God calls Abraham not for their sake alone, but for the sake of every nation. Richard Bauckham writes, "Abraham is singled out precisely so that blessing may come to all the nations, to all those seventy nations God had scattered over the face of the whole earth."[1]

The remainder of the Genesis account is the story of God's faithfulness to these promises. God is faithful to the generations of Abraham's line, despite their stubbornness, and God preserves this family's relationship to the land. As the book of Genesis closes, Jacob's household journeys to Egypt in order to escape famine. God's people become numerous in Egypt; however, they are far, far away from the land that God had promised to them.

## The Drama of the Book of Exodus

At the beginning of the book of Exodus, Pharaoh is the unopposed divine king, his rule oppressive and brutal. However, another story is unfolding. Quietly and yet powerfully, an alien God has increased the numbers of an enslaved people (Exod 1:7). This God weaves a counternarrative through slaves—through enslaved midwives, mothers, and girls. Through the cunning of brave women, God preserves and raises up Moses. Moses is exiled in Midian, and this God now speaks a word outside Egypt, where a continually burning shrub displays God's firm command of the creation. This God reveals to Moses God's name: Yahweh.

Yahweh hears the cry of the oppressed Israelites: "I ... have heard their cry" (Exod 3:7). Yahweh holds Pharaoh to account for his oppressive rule, miraculously emancipating the nation of slaves. For two and a half months the Israelites journey through the wilderness toward Sinai (Exod 15–17). In the crucible of the desert they learn to

## OUTLINE OF EXODUS

A. 1:1–6:27—Pharaoh's Oppression and Yahweh's Quiet Narrative

B. 6:28–15:21—The Plagues and the Emancipation: Yahweh the King of Justice

C. 15:22–17:16—Learning Trust on the Way to Sinai

D. 18:1–24:18—Law: A Society Reshaped as Family

E. 25:1–31—Instructions for the Tabernacle: A God Who Journeys with Us in the Muddled Mess

F. 31:12–35:3—The Golden Calf: Idolatry and Forgiveness

G. 35:4–40:38—Building the Tabernacle

trust in Yahweh for every new day. When they arrive at Mount Sinai (Exod 19), the experience of slavery is still raw: the wounds from the Egyptian whips still weep, and the horror of genocide is agonizingly fresh. At Sinai Yahweh enfolds Israel within a covenant relationship—a relationship of solidarity and of love. Yahweh gives laws in order to shape this people into a community where every member can flourish, especially the most vulnerable. There are to be no "Pharaohs" in Yahweh's society: accumulation of wealth and self-aggrandizement are expressly forbidden. Israel is to be a community of mutual care, of shared life as kindred.

At Sinai, Yahweh also gives very detailed instructions for building the tabernacle (Exod 26–31). The process of its being built is also described, in similar detail (Exod 35–40). Via the tabernacle, Yahweh pitches tent in the thick of it all, in the midst of the community, journeying with this nation in all of its muck and its mess.

> **EXODUS: BOOK AND EVENT**
>
> The exodus, when God emancipates Israel from slavery in Egypt, is the event from which the *book* of Exodus gets its name. The exodus event takes up only a small amount of space in the book. It is found in chapters 12–15, following the plagues. Nonetheless, the exodus event remains a pivotal moment in the story of God's ancient people, and it echoes throughout the biblical story. For in the exodus, God reveals the divine character as one who sides with the marginalized and oppressed; God is the Great King who challenges and defeats oppressive rulers like Pharaoh. In this event, the new nation of Israel is set on a totally different footing to the oppression of Egypt, to be a place of flourishing for all, living under Yahweh's good rule.

## How This Book Will Unfold

Here is how our journey through the book of Exodus will unfold. In chapter 1 we will see how a central motif of the book of Exodus is community. Exodus was written to transform the way that people live together in society. It is the story of how one particular people was nourished to live as a contrastive community, in the sight of the nations surrounding them. We will also think through how we as Christ-followers read the Bible as people who are called to mission, and we will tease out some implications of the book of Exodus for worshiping communities and for society today. Chapter 2 will show how the exodus event reveals God's character as one who redeems slaves, through this action birthing a new community.

Chapter 3 will unfold how the Ten Commandments shaped God's people into a community that is in total contrast to the oppression of Egypt. We will see how these commandments address some of the pressing problems of our own generation. Chapter 4 will examine the law in Exodus 21–23. Chapter 5 discusses some of the key characters in Exodus. Moses is arguably the greatest figure of the Old Testament, and we will explore his troubled and inspiring story as a case study in leadership. We then study six women who, through their strength, cunning, boldness, and decisiveness, played key roles in God's story.

In chapter 6 we learn from ancient Israel how God meets us especially in "the wilderness." In times and places of seeming hopelessness, God's people can learn to trust and to hope. In chapter 7 we focus on God, asking: If we took the picture of God in the book of Exodus seriously, what difference would it make to us? Chapter 8 will view the tabernacle and see God dwelling with humanity, up close and personal. In chapter 9 we discuss the (often difficult) theme of the judgment of God. In what ways is the judgment of God *good news*? Can we speak of God's judgment winsomely?

### SUGGESTED READING

- ☐ Genesis 3
- ☐ Genesis 12:1–3
- ☐ Genesis 47

## Reflection

What do you already know about the book of Exodus?

_____

_____

_____

What might it mean to prayerfully consider what God is inviting you into, and what God is inviting your church into, as you read the book of Exodus?

_____

_____

_____

As you move forward in this study, try to read all of Exodus.

_____

_____

_____

_____

# A COMMUNITY SHAPED FOR MISSION

## Exodus Is All About Community

The book of Exodus is all about community, about how the good news of God's kingdom transformed one small ancient Near Eastern community for the sake of the nations. In Egypt before the exodus, human relationships were deeply ruptured. Israel was "brought *out*" of slavery in Egypt in order that they might be "brought *into*" the land, so that they might live as a new kind of community, a community of kinship, of love, in communion with God. The book of Exodus is about the renewal of this community before the face of Yahweh.

This is not the way the book of Exodus is most often read, however. Individualism characterizes Western society, and we tend to read the Bible individualistically, as if it were addressed primarily to individual persons. It is as if a child receives a birthday invitation and assumes that she is the only person invited to the party. However, each book of the Bible originally addressed a community, and individuals only in the context of that community. The book of Exodus records how Yahweh was shaping God's people to live as a beloved community, in stark contrast to Egypt's oppressive society.

By way of comparison, Jesus' fellowship meals in the New Testament are another picture of the family of the kingdom of God. *Who* Jesus ate with was crucial: Jesus had a reputation for eating with those who were socially shunned, as Luke records: "The Pharisees and the scribes were grumbling and saying, 'This fellow welcomes sinners and eats with them'" (Luke 15:1–2).[2] For years I have pictured these "sinners meals" in my imagination. I have imagined Jesus' loving warmth toward this motley crew. And I have always imagined that tax collectors would have made joyful and loud company. And Jesus would have laughed with these men with a laugh full-hearted and loud! Remember, though, that Jesus didn't "invent" these fellowship meals. Rather, these meals reflect the ancient call to inclusive kinship-meals. Jesus is simply being what Israel had always been called to be!

We see this clearly in the book of Exodus. See, for example, how Yahweh addresses the *community* in three motifs: the exodus, the law, and the tabernacle.

1. *The exodus:* Yahweh sees the affliction of his people, and Yahweh hears their cry. Yahweh's compassion is for the whole community, a community of slaves. Yahweh promises to redeem Israel and to give them a land in which to dwell. Yahweh identifies as the God of their fathers, thereby showing that this people is a kinship grouping (Exod 3:7–22).

2. *The law*: We will see that the laws in Exodus were meant to shape the people to treat one another as sister-brother, as family. The laws are often addressed in the singular. For example, the Ten Commandments use the singular: in the command "You shall not steal," "you" is singular. This so called singular-address envisages the whole people of God as one cohesive community, using language to bind the people together.[3]

3. *The tabernacle*: Yahweh dwells in the midst of the people. It is with the whole people, living in community, that Yahweh dwells.

Israel was called out from their life of slavery in Egypt, and the community was brought to the foot of Sinai to become the people of God, in covenant with Yahweh. At Sinai they were called to an ongoing spiritual and ethical journey—to be an outbreak of the kingdom of God in the ancient world. Every person within this new community was to experience the freshness, the genuineness, the graciousness that flourishes when people are knit together as sisters and brothers through the redeeming activity and the loving rule of God.

## Reading Exodus Missionally

To read Exodus properly we need also to read it "missionally," to read it as people who ourselves have been sent by God for mission to our neighborhoods and places of work. There are at least two reasons for this. First, *the biblical story is the story of God's mission to God's world*. The biblical story narrates how God calls humanity back to

## EXODUS AND COMMUNITY

The book of Exodus explores themes that Christians who are seeking to live faithfully as a part of God's mission must wrestle with. Exodus prompts us to ask: What should a community of faith in the modern, Western world that is seeking to play its part in the biblical story authentically in its own place and time look like? How might such a community immerse itself in the joys and the griefs of its neighbors and its society? What does it mean today to be a community of God's people?

relationship with the Divine and how God sets about restoring every part of the creation. When God chose Abraham, the father of Israel, God promised to bless Abraham. But the blessing didn't stop there. God also said, "And in you all the families of the earth shall be blessed" (Gen 12:1-3). The whole idea of God's choosing Israel was that Israel, through their shared life of love, obedience, joy and justice, would be magnetic—that the nations would be attracted to Israel's life and see the beauty of Yahweh, Israel's God (for example, Exod 19:3-6; Deut 4:6-8).

Second, *we ourselves read the Bible as people who are called to mission.* Mission is not just one other aspect of the Christian life. Rather, mission is a part of our very identity as Christ-followers. Christ said to his disciples, "As the Father has sent me, so I send you" (John 20:21). To be Christ-followers is to be a people who are "sent". We are "sent" into our neighborhoods, cities, and places of work to live as a sign of the loving reign of God in Christ. We do this by our lives, words, and deeds. We live as an advertisement, so to speak, to this world's true king and to the joy and beauty of Christ's way. This is our very identity as Christ-followers: we are a "sent" people.

As we come to read the book of Exodus, then, we are reading a book that is *about God's mission*, as a people who *ourselves are participating in that mission*. This lens is essential, if we are to read Exodus as God intends it to be read. As Charles R. Taber comments: "Studying the Bible without seeing mission at its core is like studying the physical properties of the Statue of Liberty without noticing that it is a statue of a woman holding a torch."[4]

Let's make this personal: An Australian television program, *Bondi Rescue*, showed the work of surf lifesavers on Bondi Beach, Sydney, the day after New Year's Eve. The scene was ugly. The beach was strewn with rubbish, people had passed out in their own vomit from consuming too much alcohol, and many people were lying on the beach unconscious, getting "roasted" in the sun. Partiers who could barely stand up were risking their lives swimming. As I watched, I couldn't help thinking to myself: What if the lifesavers went off the job? What if they got drunk and became unconscious? The point for us is that there is an urgency to our missional task, and we must be vigilant. We don't stop being "sent" while we are reading the book of Exodus. Rather, *as* we read the book of Exodus, we are being shaped and energized for our missional calling. The Spirit nourishes us and shapes us as we immerse ourselves in God's word. God's word is nourishing us to live faithfully, to advertise Christ's loving rule within our neighborhood. So prepare to be shaped, challenged, and transformed. We begin by looking at the exodus event itself.

**SUGGESTED READING**

☐ Exodus 19

☐ Exodus 24

☐ Matthew 9:9–13

# Reflection

Do you tend to think of the Christian life as an individual affair, or a communal affair?

_____

_____

_____

How does relationship with God shape and influence your own Christian community?

_____

_____

_____

What difference does it make to read the Scriptures "missionally"—as the story of God's mission to God's world?

_____

_____

_____

_____

# 2

# THE EXODUS: A NEW KING AND A NEW COMMUNITY

In the film *Grand Canyon*, an attorney breaks out of a freeway traffic jam and attempts to bypass it. His route takes him along streets that become progressively darker and more deserted. Then the nightmare begins, as his car stalls in a street heavily decorated with graffiti. The lawyer phones for a tow truck, but before it arrives, five young street toughs surround his useless car and threaten him.

Just in time, the tow truck pulls up and its driver, a friendly man, begins to hook up the disabled car. The toughs protest, saying he is interrupting their fun. So, the tow truck driver takes the leader of the group aside. "Man," he says, "the world ain't supposed to work like this. Maybe you don't know that, but this ain't the way it's supposed to be. I'm supposed to be able to do my job without askin' you if I can. And that dude is supposed to be able to wait with his car without you rippin' him off. Everything's supposed to be different than what it is here."[5]

"Everything's supposed to be different than what it is here": the opening chapter of the book of Exodus moves quickly from Israel's multiplication in Egypt to their terrible oppression (Exod 1). The Israelites labored in the brick factories of Pharaoh, building the store cities of Pithom and Rameses. Many Israelites were killed or were worked to death (Exod 2:11; 5:19–21), and at the height of the atrocity Israel was subject to genocide—male babies were systematically murdered (1:16). On the one hand, this story describes a dark period in ancient Israel's unique history. On the other hand, this story is also a picture of the distortion of every human society by human evil. We well know that in every place "everything's supposed to be different than what it is here." Just consider global displacement, consider the present unprecedented inequality of wealth, and consider the grief in your own neighborhood and even in your own life.

In the exodus event, Yahweh the God of gods steps into the fray. The interpretive key for understanding the exodus event is that the ancient world was a slave culture. To have a sense of how this text would have *sounded* to the original hearers, we need to remember that the vast majority of people in the ancient world were peasant farmers, and farmers were ever in danger of going into debt and to being enslaved. Try to understand the exodus event through this lens. The terrible life of a slave was all too near for most people in the ancient world.

The following thought-chain explains the meaning of the exodus event in terms of the book of Exodus itself.

## 1. The exodus is a deliverance of Yahweh.

The exodus of Israel from Egypt is a deliverance of Yahweh. Israel does not simply leave Egypt. Rather, Israel is "brought out" by Yahweh their God.[6]

## 2. In terms of ancient law, Israel is legally freed from slavery.

Ancient Near Eastern slave laws and customs shed light on Yahweh's delivering Israel from slavery. We know from these laws that the Hebrew verb "bring out" was an ancient legal term for slave release.[7] Israel has been "brought out," legally freed, from the ownership and rule of Pharaoh, king of Egypt. This is the meaning of the phrase, "Say therefore to the Israelites, 'I am the Lord, and I will *free* you from the burdens of the Egyptians' " (Exod 6:6). Yahweh *frees* this enslaved people group.

The significance of this is enormous: the exodus is nothing short of a great act of slave emancipation. Yahweh is pictured here as the great deliverer of slaves. This most famous event, through which God's ancient people were brought into being, was Yahweh's deliverance of a downtrodden and oppressed group of people who were in the grip of the empire. In contemporary terms, the exodus was a social justice action of mammoth proportions.

### 3. Yahweh is Israel's new rightful master.

Yahweh's emancipating Israel from slavery has implications for Yahweh's relationship with the people. Yahweh becomes Israel's new, rightful master. In terms of ancient Near Eastern law and custom, as Israel's slave-redeemer Yahweh rightfully claims Israel's allegiance. A point of comparison is in an ancient Greek law code, the Law of Gortyn. In this law code, a prisoner in a foreign place who was redeemed remained the property of the one who paid the ransom until the ransom was reimbursed.[8]

So Israel has been "brought out" from under the rule of Pharaoh so that they may be "brought into" a new allegiance to Yahweh, their deliverer. Exodus signals this change of allegiance by using the same Hebrew word-root to express both Israel's identity as Pharaoh's slaves (especially in Exod 1–2) and their new identity in serving Yahweh: "Let my people go, that they may *serve* me in the wilderness" (Exod 7:16 ESV, italics added).⁹ This dynamic of a change of master is perhaps most clearly expressed in Exodus in the opening words of the Ten Commandments:

> I am the LORD your God, who brought you out of the land of Egypt, out of the house of slavery; you shall have no other gods before me. (Exod 20:2–3)

## 4. The exodus makes possible a new kind of community.

The exodus event is all about forming a new society. Israel is "brought out of slavery" in Egypt so that they may be "brought into" the promised land (Exod 12:15; 13:5) to flourish there as a renewed community. At Mount Sinai, Israel is given laws that will shape the community into a society that is totally different from the oppression of Egypt. Israel is to be a community within which every person can thrive, especially the most vulnerable. And Yahweh, the great emancipator of slaves, rules over this community in love. Exodus 19 explicitly makes this connection between Israel's exodus and their being shaped by the law into a new kind of society, in covenant relationship with God:

> You have seen what I did to the Egyptians, and how I bore you on eagles' wings and brought you to myself. Now therefore, if you obey my voice and keep my covenant, you shall be my treasured possession out of all the peoples. Indeed, the whole earth is mine, but you shall be for me a priestly kingdom and a holy nation. (Exod 19:4–6)

### 5. A compassionate king gives a compassionate law.

The law given at Sinai reflects Yahweh's own compassion and grace, the compassion with which Yahweh redeemed ancient Israel from slavery. These laws come about by a change of king. The love and mercy demonstrated in Israel's laws is possible because Yahweh is king over Israel—not Pharaoh.

## The Gift of Remembering

Healthy communities take care to remember past episodes of suffering and injustice. Australia and Canada, two countries with which I am connected, have each recently gone through a process of formally remembering how First Nations children were forcibly taken from their families and placed into institutions. The schools in which these children were forced to stay were sometimes far away from their family, and many children rarely, if ever, saw their parents. Sexual, physical, and emotional abuse was widespread in these schools. In taking the time to remember our histories, Canada and Australia have taken small steps toward healthier relationships between First Nations and settler communities. However, our process of remembering has been inadequate in very many ways, and racism and exploitation are alive and well to this very day.

In a similar way, Israel's experience in Egypt loomed large in the *memory* of the community. This memory was key to Israel's identity. It shaped what was expected of interpersonal relations and of economic relations.

## Remembering What It Was Like to Be a Stranger

One key memory was Israel's experience of being a "stranger" in Egypt (some English translations use "alien" or "sojourner"). In the time of Joseph, Jacob's family migrated to Egypt, as there was a famine in the land of Canaan (Gen 46:1-7). As a stranger, Israel was dependent on Egyptian hospitality and kindness. This memory of vulnerability prompted laws of compassion for displaced people who lived within Israel:

> You shall not wrong or oppress a stranger,
> for you were strangers in the land of Egypt.
> (Exod 22:21)

> You shall not oppress a stranger; you know
> the heart of a stranger, for you were strang-
> ers in the land of Egypt. (Exod 23:9)[10]

Israel is to offer to the stranger the kind of compassion that they themselves had desired to experience in Egypt. Israel's past as displaced people living in a foreign land equalized their relationship with outsiders in their midst. Now, everyone was a stranger—or, better, no one was a stranger! Israel's memory of being a stranger served to elicit empathy in the community for people who were on the move, seeking a home in which to survive and thrive.[11]

## Remembering What It Was Like to Be a Slave and What It Was Like to Be Redeemed

Israel's experience in Egypt became a primary motivation for the care of the most vulnerable within Israel. We shall examine the laws within the book of Exodus in more detail in the next chapter. For now, we simply observe that Israel's memory of enslavement in Egypt and of redemption was a powerful motivator for justice and compassion. One example is within a series of laws in Deuteronomy 24:

> You shall not deprive a stranger or the
> fatherless of justice; you shall not take a
> widow's garment in pledge. Remember that
> you were a slave in Egypt and the LORD your
> God redeemed you from there; therefore I
> command you to do this. ... When you gather
> the grapes of your vineyard, do not glean
> what is left; it shall be for the stranger, the
> fatherless, and the widow. Remember that

you were a slave in the land of Egypt; therefore I am commanding you to do this.
(Deut 24:17–18, 21–22[12])

Israel's liberation from slavery reveals God's character in the Old Testament. Yahweh is a god who is in the
business of freeing slaves—this is our God! Israel's God
takes sides in a situation of oppression. Yahweh sees and
hears the cry of the oppressed (Exod 3:7). God intervenes,
in power and love. This is the character of the God of gods,
our God.

Do you think of God in this way? Ancient Israel certainly did: the memory of slavery and of redemption was
a motivating impulse behind Israel's laws. Israel was to
leave the evil practices of Egypt behind them: "the LORD
your God redeemed you from there" (Deut 24:18). This
new community is to reflect the justice and compassion
of Yahweh the God of Israel. Israel was to remember,
and never to forget, their history of enslavement and of
redemption. And the word "remember" here means more
than mere cognitive memory; it means to live the kind
of shared life that is in sync with the striking reality of
Israel's history (see Exod 13:3; Deut 16:12). With the exodus
event we get a glimpse into the joyful, just, and blessed
future that God has in store not only for ancient Israel,
but also ultimately for the whole world. In this ancient
moment, the future overrides the present: Pharaoh's
oppression is judged, and a people are set free to live in
the way God intended people to live. The Lord is beginning to fulfill in this one people, Israel, the divine plans
for every people.

## CRIES OF AMAZEMENT

The exodus event displays the powerful and restoring love of God. This event has some resonances with the way in which Christ, the Son of God, walked on earth: healing lepers, making the blind see, feeding thousands, casting out demons, raising the dead, and proclaiming the rule of God, the "kingdom of God." The amazed responses to Jesus' ministry echo the singing and dancing of the Israelites after they crossed the Red Sea (Exod 15). Onlookers exclaimed:

> "What is this? A new teaching—with authority!
> He commands even the unclean spirits, and they obey him." (Mark 1:27)

> They were all amazed and glorified God, saying, "We never saw anything like this!" (Mark 2:12)

Upon crossing the Red Sea, Miriam sang:

> "Sing to the Lord, for God has triumphed gloriously;
> Throwing the horse and rider into the sea." (Exod 15:21)

Both in the exodus event and, ultimately, in Christ's life, death, and resurrection, God's rule is manifest. God's loving rule brings the world to life, and people respond with joy and astonishment. Today, God continues to rescue and restore, in order that we might live as a renewed community. The next chapter examines God's vision for community through the lens of the Ten Commandments.

**SUGGESTED READING**

☐ Exodus 1

☐ Exodus 3:1–10

☐ Exodus 12:31–51

## Reflection

What is the significance for you of the revelation of God's character in the exodus event?

_____

_____

_____

_____

What would the church be like if we took seriously this revelation of God, as the emancipator of slaves?

_____

_____

_____

_____

What would it have felt like to be a nation of freed slaves?
How might this have shaped the ethics of God's people?

_____

_____

_____

_____

# 3

# THE LAW COLLECTION

## Introduction

At the heart of the book of Exodus, between the story of redemption (chapters 1–17) and the building of the tabernacle (chapters 25–40), stands the law. The law is deeply connected to the book's story. God has redeemed Israel from slavery in Egypt, and less than three months later, at Mount Sinai, God gives the law to Israel. God has rescued Israel in order that Israel may live as a contrastive community, as a light to the nations (Isa 42:6). So the giving of the law is a crowning moment in God's grace. It is a bit like my friend Maria, who received refugee status in Canada and has since dedicated the rest of her life to helping other asylum seekers. The relief that Maria has experienced in her own life invigorates her to pursue justice for others. We might say that Israel is a "so that" people: Israel is redeemed *so that* God may extend grace to all people.

Israel's life of love is not self-acquired holiness. Nor is it an effort at moral achievement. Rather, God has emancipated Israel, and now calls and empowers the community to embrace the freedom of the exodus. It is as if the exodus event has opened a gate that leads into a lush garden, a garden that represents a new community. Israel is invited to enjoy that garden, tending to its plants responsibly (obeying the law) and feasting on its fruits. This is why the psalmist delights in the law, singing:

> With my lips I declare
>> all the ordinances of your mouth.
> I delight in the way of your decrees
>> as much as in all riches. (Ps 119:13-14)

Through the exodus event God gives Israel a new identity. In this way, we can understand how the law is an expression of God's grace to Israel. We have already seen that, by redeeming the Israelites from slavery, Yahweh has become their new master. At Sinai, where Yahweh makes a covenant with Israel, Yahweh says, "You shall be for me a priestly kingdom and a holy nation" (Exod 19:6). As a "holy nation," Israel is set apart from the other nations as those who belong to the Lord and who are given a specific task. As a "kingdom of priests," Israel exists for the sake of blessing the nations: Israel is to be the conduit through which Yahweh extends blessing to every people. Within this new identity, the law shapes Israel to live as a contrastive community.

There are three main law collections in the Pentateuch (the "Pentateuch" is the first five books of the Old Testament). They are found in Exodus 21:1-23:19, Leviticus 17-25, and Deuteronomy 12-26. This present chapter explores the law collection of Exodus, and the next chapter examines the Ten Commandments (Exod 20:1-17). Even though the Ten Commandments precede the law collection in Exodus, we will study the law collection first in order to give us a fresh lens through which to read the Ten Commandments.

## Interpreting Law

How are we to interpret the laws of the Pentateuch? The traditional Protestant way of interpreting the Old Testament law views the law as a kind of spotlight that casts its light around our lives, displaying our sinfulness. Martin Luther stressed that it is impossible to keep the law in its entirety. He said that humanity is like an ill patient who is overconfident and who will not admit to being ill. And the law is like a doctor, who may tell this patient to do something that is impossible or painful in order to make the patient aware of their illness.[13] Certainly, the law has this role of making us aware of our sinfulness and of our need for Christ. However, there is more to be said. By itself, this way of interpreting the law sidesteps the primary reason why the law was given in the first place.

The missional dimension of the book of Exodus assists us to interpret the laws for all that they are worth. The law was to shape Israel to reflect God's original intention for community. Shaped by the law, this community was to reject the brutal and accumulative politics of Egypt. Lesslie Newbigin describes the function of the law helpfully:

> Israel was the Lord's garden, a small oasis of cleanness and beauty in the midst of a world which is a desert of idolatry and the chaos of wickedness. And the hedge which protected this garden, was the Law.[14]

The law shaped Israel into a contrast-community that lived in the sight of the nations, bearing witness through its transformed life to the loving reign of God. This was a breaking in of the kingdom of God into human society that was in the thrall of evil. The law was an instrument of the Spirit, through which God worked in power to bring healing to human relationships.

To put it another way, in Scripture, God's reign is never felt *only* in people's hearts. To be sure, God's reign is felt in our hearts. In Old Testament times people communed with God in prayer, in song, in lament, and in praise, with their hearts devoted to God (for example, Ps 130). However, where God reigns, *everything* changes! God's healing power goes deep down into every aspect of human life: into human relationships, into the structure of society, into politics, into eating practices, into the law courts, and into economics. The law is an invitation to live well, in community with one another.

These laws were addressed specifically to Israel, and they were carefully tailored to fit the particular needs of this small and ancient nation. However, these laws also had implications for every nation, for Israel's God is the God of gods. Yahweh declares at Sinai: "The whole earth is mine, but you shall be for me a priestly kingdom and a holy nation" (Exod 19:5–6). Exodus was a covenant document between Yahweh and one particular kingdom, Israel, which disclosed Yahweh's desire for every kingdom.

We learn from these laws principles and directions that are relevant for every community in every era. Perhaps this is like watching a reality-TV cooking contest. The judge's comments on one poor chef's cooking disaster are specific to that particular dish. However, from the judge's comments the viewers can learn principles and lessons for cooking that are relevant for the meals that we *all* cook—even if we never cook that particular dish.

## SIX STEPS FOR INTERPRETING BIBLICAL LAW

How then do we consider these ancient laws for communities today? Here is a six-step method for reading these laws. You might like to take some time to work through these six steps with one or two of the laws discussed in the next section.

A. What was the original function of the law, in the setting for which it was written?[15] Consider what ancient social issues this law may have been addressing. What might it have looked like to obey the law within the culture for which the laws were written?

B. What is the objective of the law, which applies across cultures? What does this law teach us about how humanity is to live together or about how we are to relate to God? These objectives also apply today.

C. Literary sensitivity: is there anything in the way that this law is expressed that stands out to you? Is anything emphasized? Is there any repetition?

D. We ourselves read Scripture as a community that is caught up in God's story for his world. What is the invitation in the text for your own ‑shiping community?

‑t cultural idols does this law challenge
‑y?

‑ere a prophetic challenge to society
‑/?

Similarly, in these ancient laws we can discern God's heart for how humanity is to live together in community, and that has implications for our own community.

## Three Kinds of Law

The law collection of Exodus contains three kinds of law:

1. *Statutory law* (Exod 21:1–22:16). The statutory laws address various hypothetical legal cases, balancing the needs of the perpetrator and the victim.

2. *Cultic law* (Exod 20:24–26; 22:17–19), concerning the worship of Yahweh.

3. *Social law* (Exod 22:20–23:9). This law is concerned with protecting the most vulnerable in the community.

### Statutory law

Perhaps the most troubling of the statutory laws concerns situations where a daughter is sold as a slave.

> When a man sells his daughter as a slave, she shall not go out as the male slaves do. If she does not please her master, who designated her for himself, then he shall let her be redeemed; he shall have no right to sell her to a foreign people, since he has dealt unfairly with her. If he designates her for his son, he shall deal with her as with a daughter. If he takes another wife to himself, he shall not diminish the food, clothing, or marital rights of the first wife. And if he does not do these three things for her, she shall go out

without debt, without payment of money.
(Exod 21:7–11)

Faced with starvation and indebtedness, a family may need to sell their daughter as a slave. Such a family would be so impoverished that the normal process for marriage isn't available to their daughter. In this inhumane scenario, the daughter may become, in effect, the wife of her new master. Yet, without the usual exchange of dowry, this is a very different kind of marriage: a woman in these circumstances has lower status and less protection. This law protects the rights of a young woman under these circumstances.

This law contains three scenarios: In the first scenario, Exodus 21:7–8, the woman remains a virgin. In this situation, the law provides that she may be redeemed (bought back) by the family. The phrase, "he shall have no right to sell her to a foreign people" (v. 8), is probably evidence of sex trade in this period; such a practice is forbidden. In the second scenario, Exodus 21:9, the woman becomes the wife of the master's son. In such a case, she must be treated as one of the family. In the third scenario, the woman's marital rights and human rights are protected.[16] The upshot of these three stipulations is that a daughter who is sold to pay off a debt must be treated with dignity, as a member of the family. After all, the exodus event has shown that Yahweh does not desire that any person remain as a slave.

## Cultic law

Among the cultic laws in the book of Exodus is provision for three festivals (Exod 23:14–17): the Festival of Unleavened Bread, the Festival of the Harvest (also called the Festival of Weeks), and the Festival of Ingathering (also called the Festival of Booths). Through the Festival of Unleavened Bread, the community ritualizes and embodies the exodus event, specifically remembering Yahweh's judgment upon their Egyptian oppressors:

> As I commanded you, you shall eat unleavened bread for seven days at the appointed time in the month of Abib, for in it you came out of Egypt. (Exod 23:14)

Through the Festival of the Harvest and the Festival of Ingathering, the community celebrates the harvest as God's generous supply. Through these festivals, the community is re-narrated, as it were, into God's story of redemption and provision. They are reminded of their identity as God's beloved community and of their responsibility to extend God's blessings to every person within the community.

## Social law

In what follows we tease out the implications of the *social* laws in the book of Exodus.

### The Stranger

A "stranger" in Israel (this is also translated as "alien" or "sojourner" in some English Bibles) was someone who had been displaced from their extended family (their clan) and from the land that they were traditionally connected with. Such people were vulnerable to starvation and could be indebted and enslaved, for they had no land, resources, or kindred to protect them. Yahweh demanded that such people be protected from exploitation:

> You shall not wrong or oppress a stranger,
> for you were strangers in the land of Egypt
> (Exod 22:21).

> You shall not oppress a stranger; you know
> the heart of a stranger, for you were strang-
> ers in the land of Egypt. (Exod 23:9)[17]

We might compare these with a law from Deuteronomy:

> Yahweh executes justice for the fatherless
> and the widow, and loves the stranger, giving
> them food and clothing. Love the stranger,
> therefore, for you were strangers in the land
> of Egypt. (Deut 10:18–19, author's translation)

Strangers were employed on farms and in households, and they had to be treated with compassion and paid fairly. Their freedom could not be taken from them.

As I am writing this, large numbers of homeless and vulnerable people from Syria, Afghanistan, Somalia, and elsewhere are struggling to survive in camps, at borders, and in transit. The numbers of people displaced from their homes are unprecedented in human history—no less than 79.5 million people at the time of writing. Some of these people are displaced internally, in their own country. And, some 35 million people have been displaced across national borders. God's heart for displaced people is expressed clearly and emphatically in these laws. To be sure, a generous welcome for asylum seekers may be costly—for now the world is shot through with imbalances and dysfunctions, and justice doesn't come easily. Nonetheless, God's deep compassion for people who are experiencing vulnerability is made known in the exodus event—a compassion that we see so clearly in Christ. God's compassion is made specific in these laws: we are to welcome the stranger. Is there an invitation here for your own worshiping community? To offer a practical example, our church has given birth to Kinbrace Refugee Housing and Support, an organization that has been providing housing and support for refugee claimants for over twenty years. Other churches have engaged in refugee sponsorship or in providing housing or education for newcomers.

## The Fatherless and the Widow

> You shall not mistreat any widow or fatherless child. If you do mistreat them, when they cry out to me, I will surely heed their cry, and my wrath will burn, and I will kill you with the sword, and your wives shall become widows and your children fatherless. (Exod 22:22–24)

The fatherless and the widow were the poorest of the poor in the ancient Near East. These people were separated from the protection that male family members could offer. The fatherless and the widow were especially vulnerable to starvation and exploitation.

Evildoers should beware that Yahweh's ears are especially attuned to the voice of the poor: "If you do abuse them, when they cry out to me, I will surely heed their cry; my wrath will burn" (Exod 22:23–24). Readers today should not underestimate the force of God's assertion: "when they cry out to me, I will surely heed their cry." This verse is not isolated. A number of such statements show that God is particularly attentive to the voice of the poor (see also Deut 24:13, 15). God's attentiveness to vulnerable people is a bit like a parent who, in a room full of children, recognizes the crying voice of their own child (compare Matt 25:31–46). And this shouldn't surprise us, as it was the cry of the oppressed Israelites that spurred Yahweh to intervene in Pharaoh's oppressive regime (Exod 3:7–10).

What is your response to this? Is this a new picture of God for you? Perhaps you yourself can experience God's grace by seeking God's heart, revealed in these laws. Practically speaking, in the school your children attend,

## INSIGHTS FROM THE HEBREW TEXT

The Hebrew word that is translated "widow" in Exodus is *almanah*. This was "a woman without males who [were] responsible for supporting her."[18] Not every widow was an *almanah*. Upon the death of her husband, the responsibility for a women's sustenance fell on her sons (of a suitable age) or on her father-in-law. If the woman had no male kin with the obligation for her protection and support, then she became an *almanah*.

The Hebrew word *yatom* is generally translated as "orphan"; however, "fatherless" is more accurate. The father was the legal representative of the child in the ancient Near East and in ancient Israel. The absence of a responsible male left a child without a legal identity.[19] The *yatom* may have a surviving mother, and a *yatom* without either parent was in an especially perilous situation. In the ancient Near East it was common enough for households to entrap the poor and to force them to provide cheap labor. Yahweh, however, forbids such practices: "You shall not mistreat any widow or fatherless child" (Exod 22:22, author's translation).

is there a lonely family you can befriend? Is there an individual who is lonely or isolated to whom you can offer kinship? Are there people living in your neighborhood to whom your church can offer creative support?

### Loans without Interest (Exodus 22:25)

> If you lend money to my people, to the poor among you, you shall not deal with them as a creditor; you shall not exact interest from them. (Exod 22:25)

Common practice in the ancient Near East was to lend money or grain to peasant households who had fallen on hard times. This loan would enable farmers to sow a new crop. Failure to repay both the capital and the interest at the harvest time could mean that members of the household became debt slaves. Because of the high interest rate on debts, the poor had little chance to escape their poverty. This law in Exodus stipulated that no-interest loans be offered to God's people in times of need. People of means must use their wealth not to gain more wealth but to assist those in need. This turned the standard practice on its head, insisting that wealth not be hoarded but shared among God's people.

Consider: What implications might there be for our practices as Christ-followers? What, in light of this law, are we to think about the massive global disparity of wealth? During the time of writing this book, for the first time the world's richest 1 percent own more than the rest of the 99 percent.[20] These laws should prompt Christians to think creatively about addressing income inequality. We may do this at a personal level, using our household income for the sake of others. Can we move beyond prioritizing buying a lovely house and funding fancy holidays, to be generous and even creative with our incomes? As churches, how can we take initiative for the sake of people with low incomes in our neighborhood? And at a political level, how can we advocate for public policy that addresses income inequity?

## Pledges (Exodus 22:26–27)

> If you take your neighbor's cloak in pledge,
> you shall restore it before the sun goes down;
> for it may be your neighbor's only clothing to
> use as cover; in what else shall that person
> sleep? And, if your neighbor cries out to me,
> I will listen, for I am compassionate. (Exod
> 22:26–27, author's translation)

In ancient times, an impoverished person may have given their outer garment to another person as security, in order that they could take out a short-term loan. Say a person receives their wages in the morning, before the day's work, so that they can feed their family. They might well give over their outer garment as a pledge against this loan. However, the outer garment was a vital piece of clothing, doubling as a protection from rain during the day and a blanket at night. The prophet Amos denounced the practice of taking an outer garment as security against a loan: "They lay themselves down beside every altar on garments taken in pledge" (Amos 2:8). In the law above, Exodus states that the garment of an impoverished person must be returned before sundown.

This law teaches that economically poor people must be treated with dignity and compassion. Profit doesn't have the final word; human dignity and flourishing is a priority. This law also dignifies the impoverished person by referring to them as "your neighbor." Theologically this law is grounded in the compassionate character and actions of Yahweh.

In our day, this biblical ethic of protecting and empowering people who have less challenges global financial practices between richer and poorer countries. Economists have shown that significantly more money flows from developing countries to developed countries than the other way—more than double the amount. For example, the interest payments servicing debt that developing countries pay to developed countries far exceeds the amount that developing countries receive in aid from developed counties. Some writers have concluded that "poor countries develop rich countries."[21] The biblical law of Exodus sharply challenges this pattern.

### Law Courts (Exodus 23:1–8)

One of the biggest snares for impoverished or displaced people in the ancient world was the legal system. Whether they were standing before an official judge within a city or before the local village elders, poorer people often faced many obstacles as they sought to obtain justice. The needy lacked influential advocates. Officials were appointed from influential families, and they enjoyed a network of relationships with the elite. In this context, the Egyptian ruler Thutmose III described the qualities of a just judge to his vizier Rekhmire, naming explicitly the temptation to show partiality. Here are the qualities of a just judge:

> He is the one who does not make himself a friend of anyone. ... It is an abomination to God to show partiality. This is an instruction. ... Regard him whom you know like him whom you do not know.[22]

Exodus 23:1–8 is a lengthy tirade against biased legal process. People who exert their power in order to influence judicial processes must be resisted (23:1, 7). The poor, in particular, are to be protected in their lawsuits: "Nor shall you be partial to the poor in a lawsuit" (23:3, author's translation).

In most, if not all, countries today, vulnerable people have far less recourse to just legal processes than well-to-do people. Consider the widespread US practice of moving detained immigrants and refugees between states with the result that they cannot have consistent legal representation. Or consider that all asylum seekers arriving on Australian shores by boat are removed offshore and denied their right to apply for refugee status—an action that has been declared illegal by the United Nations high commissioner for refugees. The book of Exodus displays for us God's heart for just legal processes for vulnerable people. Of course, God's heart has not changed. (Do we not see the compassion of Christ in the Gospels, as well as Christ's outrage at those who are either indifferent to suffering or else active in perpetrating evil?[23]) These laws can spur the church on to seek just legal procedure for those who do not have access to it. Here is an example of what this might look like: Ebony Birchall is a gifted and compassionate Christian lawyer in Sydney, Australia. God provided a wonderful opportunity for her to play a key role in a successful lawsuit against the Australian government for its policy of detaining refugees and asylum seekers in offshore detention facilities in deplorable conditions.[24] Other Christian lawyers sacrifice time and money in order to provide *pro bono* legal assistance to vulnerable people.

## Missional Implications, Then and Now

I am a jazz pianist and for many years eked out a (very meager) living as a professional jazz musician. In a sense, Israel was to live in the way of an excellent jazz quartet—harmonious, creative, and valuing the contribution of every person. These were the sounds of God's good creation, in the beginning. The "music" of Israel's cultural environment was mass-produced by the empires of Egypt, Assyria, Babylon, and Persia. These empires were brutal, taxing Israel and its neighbors without pity and funneling the wealth to the center. Israel's own kings were always tempted to reign like the pharaohs, in effect returning Israel to Egypt (Deut 17:16).

Today, in the basements of every Western city, jazz music flourishes. Jazz sings in the shadow of an "empire" of corporatized sounds—of deafening traffic and reality-TV pop music. In the arts world, jazz invites us to recover our roots, to remember our humanity, to remember racism and the suffering of African American people, and to rest. In a similar way, Israel was to improvise a new kind of harmonious life, by living together as kindred. The weakest among them were to be brought into the center of the community. Israel was to play its tunes amid the harsh and alluring tones of the empire. Its music was a testimony to the wisdom and beauty of the lead player, Yahweh.

In the next chapter we tease out some of the implications of Israel's law for worshiping communities today by examining the Ten Commandments.

**SUGGESTED READING**

☐ Exodus 22:21–23:9

☐ Leviticus 19

☐ Deuteronomy 24

## Reflection

What was your impression of the law in the Old Testament before reading this chapter? What is your impression of the law now?

_____

_____

_____

_____

Does the Old Testament law affect your thinking on public policy in any way?

_____

_____

_____

_____

How does the Old Testament law speak into the question of welcoming asylum-seekers in your country?

_____

_____

_____

_____

# 4

# TEN COMMANDMENTS

## Introduction to the Ten Commandments

In the previous chapter we got a "feel" for the nature of the law in Exodus. We also considered a method for interpreting the law. We now turn to the most famous section of biblical law of all, the Ten Commandments. The Ten Commandments have been cherished in every era of the church up until now. John Calvin, the most prominent theologian of the sixteenth-century Reformation period, understood the Ten Commandments as an expression of the divine law, stipulating both what is owed to God and what is owed to our fellow humans.[25] As an old man, Martin Luther, another sixteenth-century Reformer, said: "I recite the Ten Commandments daily word for word like a child."[26]

However, it is probably fair to say that these days the Ten Commandments don't receive much attention. After all, they can seem somewhat irrelevant. We read, "You shall not murder," and we think, "I haven't murdered!" Or we read, "You shall not steal," and we think, "I haven't stolen!" So, aren't the Ten Commandments written to confront *really* wicked people? Today the Ten Commandments tend to be interpreted and preached on individualistically, focusing on personal piety, and this increases the sense of their irrelevance, at least for millennials. The Ten Commandments don't seem to address global and cultural issues.

Few Christians realize that the pressing problems of our generation—for example, massive inequality of wealth, growing refugee populations, and rampant consumerism—are issues that the Ten Commandments address stridently. In their original context, they were a platform for justice arising out of a deep reverence for God and communion with God. And they can play this role today. For our generation, recovering the Ten Commandments will equip the church to live gratefully, generously, and prophetically. They will give us fresh reasons to worship our great God.

The Ten Commandments appear twice in the Old Testament in their full form, in Exodus 20:1–17 and in Deuteronomy 5:1–21. These laws were first given from Mount Sinai less than three months after the exodus from Egypt. They were delivered to Israel a second time one generation later, in Moab on the edge of the Jordan River just before Israel entered the promised land.

## The Setting of the Ten Commandments

To understand the Ten Commandments properly we have to remember that these rules were received by Israel shortly after they were rescued from slavery in Egypt across the Red Sea. The Israelites arrived at Mount Sinai to receive these Ten Words with the wounds on their back from Egyptian whips still raw and open.

Consider what life had been like for the Israelites in Egypt before God delivered them. The Hebrews labored in the brick factories of Pharaoh. Under the whip, they built store cities for Pharaoh: Pithom and Rameses (Exod 1:11). When brick quotas weren't met, Israelite foremen were beaten, often, doubtless, to death (5:16). Remember when Moses intervened as a Hebrew slave was beaten (2:11)? That's no children's story. Remember, too, the policy that amounted to genocide, that male babies were systematically destroyed to reduce the threat of an uprising (1:15–22). Chilling also is Pharaoh's command that the Israelites must make bricks and also gather their own straw for the bricks (5:1–23). Pharaoh ignored the Israelite foremen's plea that this task is impossible. Pharaoh's insufferable command is a virtual death sentence: these workers will either die trying to fulfill it or else be beaten to death when they fail to deliver. The narrator writes: "The Israelite supervisors saw that they were in trouble when they were told, 'You shall not lessen your daily number of bricks'" (5:19). Lives—Israelite lives, at least—were expendable in the economic expansion of Pharaoh. Economic productivity was god.

God strategically placed one Hebrew, Moses, in the courts of the empire. And one day, by a burning bush, God said to Moses:

> I have observed the misery of my people
> who are in Egypt; I have heard their cry
> on account of their taskmasters. Indeed, I
> know their sufferings, and I have come down

> to deliver them from the Egyptians, and to
> bring them up out of that land to a good and
> broad land, a land flowing with milk and
> honey, to the country of the Canaanites, the
> Hittites, the Amorites, the Perizzites, the
> Hivites, and the Jebusites. (Exod 3:7–8)

Yahweh the God of Israel came and emancipated this enslaved people. Yahweh brought the Israelites to Mount Sinai to meet with him. As we come to study the Ten Commandments now, we will see that with these laws God is creating a new community that operates how God wants communities to operate—a place where every person can thrive, a community transformed from a society of whips and slaughter to a society of mutual care.

Yahweh writes these commandments on two stone tablets. Broadly speaking, the first four commands are concerned with the exclusive worship of Yahweh. The remaining six commands are concerned with how the Israelites are to live in community with one another. Throughout the remainder of this chapter, we will unpack five of the commandments and then draw some conclusions for the church today.

## The First Commandment: Exclusive Worship

With the first commandment, Yahweh demands Israel's exclusive worship. "You shall have no other gods before my face," the Hebrew text reads literally. As God of gods, Yahweh will not share the divine throne room with any other deity. No other god may compete for Israel's allegiance—neither the "great" gods who stand behind the great empires, nor the minor personal gods who are thought to protect an individual household. Yahweh's covenant with Israel requires absolute allegiance: Israel is to have no other gods.

The revelation of God in Exodus—the fire, the powerful acts, the law, and so on—required Israel's awe and reverence. And yet there is also deep tenderness and compassion within this divine/human relationship. Yahweh says: "I bore you on eagles' wings and brought you to myself" (Exod 19:4). God dwelled *among* the people (25:8); Yahweh is Israel's healer (15:26).

The first commandment also has ethical implications. Immediately preceding the first command is, "I am the LORD your God, who brought you out of the land of Egypt, out of the house of slavery" (Exod 20:2-3; Deut 5:6). Yahweh is revealed to the people as the God who intervenes for the sake of the most vulnerable—as opposed to the great gods of Egypt, who sponsored Pharaoh and his regime.

## The Fourth Commandment: Sabbath Rest

In Egypt there was no weekly day of rest, especially for the Israelites. The brick factories of Pharaoh did not stop for weekends. But God said:

> Remember the sabbath day, and keep it holy.
> Six days you shall labor and do all your work.
> But the seventh day is a sabbath to the LORD
> your God; you shall not do any work—you,
> your son or your daughter, your male or
> female slave, your livestock, or the stranger
> in your towns. For in six days the LORD made

> heaven and earth, the sea, and all that is in
> them, but rested the seventh day; therefore
> the LORD blessed the Sabbath day and con-
> secrated it. (Exod 20:8–11)[27]

A weekly day of rest is proclaimed for a nation of slaves. What a relief! If a person is to thrive, life must consist of more than work. We need space for rest and for play. No one in Israel, especially vulnerable people and even the animals, was to be deprived of this rhythm of work and rest, work and rest, work and rest.

The Sabbath command injects a life-giving pause into the endless cycle of production. Egypt had a policy of production at any cost. In Israel, however, the flourishing of all human beings was a priority. The most vulnerable people in the community, slaves and strangers, were not to be exploited for their labor. These too were to share in the Sabbath rest. In this way, the Sabbath command dignifies the most vulnerable as full members of the society and as participants in the community. The gifts of God are for these people, too.

What does the Sabbath mean for Christians today? It teaches us that we must not live in such a way that other people cannot rest. It prompts us to explore creative ways to foster for vulnerable people their full participation in the community. It teaches us too that the earth must rest (Exod 23:10–11).

Here is a practical example of how a worshiping community might live into the Sabbath command. Our church has developed an agency called Just Work that seeks to give dignifying work to people who find it difficult to hold down a permanent job because of disability or some other misfortune. Just Work offers supported employment in renovation work, in catering, and in pottery—a pottery studio is located in the basement of our church building. Through this dignifying work, our friends enter into the Sabbath rhythm of work and rest. Just Work shifts the goalposts of economic production. The bottom line is twofold: twin goals to both produce revenue and create dignifying work.

The Sabbath command also prompts us to think seriously about climate change. Climate change is arguably the most significant political and social issue today, by virtue of its sheer irreversibility. In low-lying areas, the world's poorest families are already being forced off their land. The Pacific island nation of Kiribati, for example, will almost certainly become completely submerged in a matter of years.[28] The Sabbath command, however, injects a life-giving pause in the endless cycle of production. It demands that the people of Kiribati are able to rest on their own land. And it demands that the earth itself can rest (Exod 23:10-11).

By the time of the first century, the Sabbath had lost its original ethical impulse. Jesus challenged the rule-bound application of the Sabbath that was expounded by some Jewish leaders of his day: "'I ask you, is it lawful to do good or to do harm on the Sabbath, to save life or to destroy it?'" (Luke 6:9; see also Matt 23:23; Mark 2:27; Luke 13:16; 14:1-6).[29]

## The Sixth Commandment: "You Shall Not Murder"

Now, let's skip over to the sixth commandment, "You shall not murder." This law today tends to be applied individualistically: murder is a crime. It has also been applied across all of society—to capital punishment, to abortion, and to war. These implications of the sixth command are important, though they are also complex.

The command "You shall not murder" also has implications restraining the excesses of powerful people, such as Pharaoh, for the background for this law is slavery in Egypt. What beautiful words these are to give to this nation of bereaved families and endangered brick workers. Human life is valued! In Egypt, economic productivity was valued more highly than human life: the foreman's life was threatened for the sake of brick quotas; male babies were killed to keep the labor force in subjugation. Unlike Egypt, Israel is not to be an economy of production at any cost but an economy of neighborly well-being.

This interpretation of the sixth command is established also by numerous biblical laws that prioritize human life over the accumulation of wealth. For example, here is another law concerning pledges:

> No one shall take a mill or an upper millstone
> in pledge, for that would be taking a life in
> pledge. (Deut 24:6)

An upper millstone was used to grind the grain for making bread, and so households depended on this tool for survival—for their very life. Therefore, a creditor was not permitted to carry away an upper millstone as security against a loan.

Israel's law is radical here. In too many societies, economic productivity is subtly valued more highly than human life. In England two hundred years ago, a person was hanged if they stole a sheep. In this context, economic production was valued more highly than human life. The sixth command should prompt you to consider the ways in which your culture might be tolerating a similar value reversal. One sphere where this may be the case is international trade. Canada, where I live, collects about half its tariff revenue from developing countries. This makes the products from developing countries more expensive to purchase. These tariffs are often much higher than the tariffs charged on imported goods from, for example, New Zealand or the United States, countries from whom Canada might benefit. As a result of colonial history and ongoing trade practices, among other dynamics, the world's poorest countries have been left behind in any advancements made by globalization and technology—indeed the wealth disparity between nations is growing.[30]

The sixth commandment teaches us that God has an opinion about unjust trade rules: human life takes priority over economic gain. In the Old Testament, the value of human life is grounded in this way: "Whoever sheds the blood of a human, by a human shall that person's blood be shed; for in God's own image God made humankind" (Gen 9:6). People are made in God's image; therefore, "You shalt not murder."

## Eighth Commandment: "You Shall Not Steal"

We are going to skip over the seventh commandment and go to the eighth, "You shall not steal." For most of my life, this command brought to my mind an image of a thief in a black mask creeping around a house at night. In my imagination the thief was wearing a black-and-white striped shirt, like the Hamburgler from McDonalds. I suppose that I was imagining someone who was poor stealing from someone who was rich.

This is true, in a sense, for the eighth command forbids any kind of theft. However, the command "You shall not steal" was given primarily to restrain the rich.[31] Consider, for example, the biblical laws surrounding land possession. Land law was the main protection against poverty in Israel. Every Israelite family was to own land. The land was used for agriculture and for grazing. We learn from the book of Joshua that the land was divided up among the Israelites so that every family had this means of production. Land ownership could not be revoked by anyone, according to Israelite law. God says: "The land must not be sold permanently, because the land is mine" (Lev 25:23 NIV). God owns the land, and has given everybody some of it. What a remarkable economic arrangement! Wealth producing capital is in the hands of every Israelite—not in the hands of a privileged few.

This means that no Israelite family can permanently fall into poverty, and, no one family can accumulate excessively. The accumulation of wealth by powerful people like Pharaoh is prohibited. We can express the primary intention of this command with these two points:

☐ This command secures God's gift of land to each household.

☐ This command restrains excessive accumulation on the part of one household at the expense of others.

We could summarize the spirit of the eighth command with the words of Craig Blomberg: "God owns it all, and wants everybody to enjoy some of it."[32] We should celebrate that God has given us enough not only to live but also to share.

The eighth command has an invitation to worshiping communities today: be a community that is committed to living simply. In our experience here in Vancouver, British Columbia, it is almost impossible not to be influenced by the wealth and the lifestyle of our neighbors. It is extremely challenging for an individual or a family to say no to the pressures of consumerism. But together as a community of God's people indwelt by the Spirit and encouraging each other, there are real possibilities. It can even be a rich joy! In one church where I pastored, we shared in an annual month of gratitude. We were invited to step away from our habits of consumption by committing to one specific change for a month. Some people committed to making only food purchases and nothing else. Others didn't eat out for a month. One family lived on a food budget of $2 per person, per day, in order to share in the experience of the one-third of the global population that lives in poverty. This month reshaped our expectations for the rest of the year so that we were content to live with less.

The command "you shall not steal" also invites us to consider what it means to pursue profit. Businesspeople who seek to live faithfully into the biblical story may consider ways they can share their profit. For example, the social enterprise that I mentioned above, Just Work, seeks both to provide employment for people who are not able to find stable employment and to produce revenue from the various contracts that it fulfills in order to maintain its viability as an organization.

## Tenth Commandment: You Shall Not Covet

Looking at the tenth commandment might help us clear up one of the biggest misunderstandings that Christians have about the Old Testament. People often think the Old Testament is all about rules. Others find it boring and irrelevant. Do you ever think that way about the Old Testament? But observe the change of heart that God desires from Israel in the tenth commandment:

> You shall not covet your neighbor's house;
> you shall not covet your neighbor's wife,
> or male or female slave, or ox, or donkey,
> or anything that belongs to your neighbor.
> (Exod 20:17)

This isn't legislation; this is stuff of the heart. This command is intended to foster a desire that our fellow human beings would thrive. To covet is to want something even if it disadvantages another person; however, that path is forbidden in Israel.

In practical terms, this is what it might have looked like in ancient Israel: Say my neighbor has fallen into hard times. And say he wants to sell me his ox, his only ox, so that he can buy some grain. The point of the tenth commandment is that I don't take him for all he's worth—I don't covet his ox, and I don't covet his money. I trade in a way that is helpful to him and generous to him. And if he doesn't have an ox to sell, then I should give him some of my grain anyway.

This command calls Israelites to something higher than just rules. It calls them out of an attitude of acquisition (the spirit of Pharaoh) and into a spirit of mutual care. This spirit is to infuse the whole nation of Israel so that the people live together as kindred, in kindness, in humility, and in love.

## Conclusion: The Weakest in the Center

I first began to read the Ten Commandments in their original context, as I have done here, when I was pastoring in a government housing area in Western Sydney, Australia. Today, this neighborhood continues to be rich in community and yet relatively poor in wealth and in employment. I learned some important lessons during that time. I learned that many single mothers have no time for paid work, and a government reduction in welfare payments means that many mothers literally can't afford both food and housing. During this period, I also learned more about how indigenous children in Australia were forcibly taken from their families and put into mission schools. I learned that this had been the childhood ___ ny of my neighbors and friends. Putting all this ___ w that human suffering is not caused only by ___ but also by societal systems. The people on the bottommost rung of the economic ladder, whether locally or globally, are usually not there by choice but by misfortune. And the various structures within a society, whether accidentally or deliberately, operate to keep them there.

Living as a part of this community, I began to read certain parts of Scripture afresh, including the Ten Commandments. I began to realize that God's desire for humanity also includes the ways in which we live with one another in society. Even as God stakes claim to the heart of every person, God also stakes claim to the societies that people create: to economics, to community, to poverty, to urban planning, to welfare, to social services, to employment, to trade, to the environment, to media, to the use of technology, to construction, to racism, to equality, to immigration, and to education. In all of these spheres of society, the Father desires that his will be done on earth as it is in heaven.

The Ten Commandments are an ancient and poignant expression of God's will for society. It is also a stark expression of this will. Two powerful characters, standing in opposition, have left their mark on the Ten Commandments: Yahweh the God of Israel and Pharaoh the king of Egypt (who thought that he was a god). All ten of the commandments stand as a rebuke to Pharaoh and his regime in one way or another.

Also, two models for society stand in opposition to each other. One is a society of profit at any cost, the way of Pharaoh. The other is a society that lives as family, the way of Yahweh. This diagram represents these two rulers and these two societies.

## Two Models for Society

| **Judged and left behind** | | **A brand new day** |
|---|---|---|
| *Organizer:*<br>Pharaoh |  | *Organizer:*<br>Yahweh |
| *Model for society:*<br>Accumulation and consolidated power | | *Model for society:*<br>Kinship |

The model for societies of accumulation and consolidated power is judged and left behind in the exodus event. God's good rule opens the potential for a brand-new day for human relationships, where humanity lives as family.

We have seen God's vision for human society in Israel's law; now we take a close look at some of the significant figures in the book of Exodus whom God used to accomplish this vision.

**SUGGESTED READING**

☐ Exodus 20:1–18

☐ Isaiah 58–59

☐ Luke 14:1–24

## Reflection

What is the difference between how the Ten Commandments are understood in your worshiping community and their original intention?

_____

_____

_____

_____

What is one example of structural injustice in your neighborhood that your worshiping family could address together?

_____

_____

_____

What might be the first step toward addressing this issue?

_____

_____

_____

_____

# 5

# MOSES AND THE WOMEN WHO TRICKED PHARAOH

In this chapter we see the lives of people who were used powerfully by God in the work of the kingdom. The book of Exodus offers Moses as a model of persevering and loving leadership. Exodus also celebrates a number of women who by their strength and cunning contributed to Pharaoh's downfall.

## A Portrait of a Leader: Moses in Exodus

### Moses' Early Years

Moses is a standout Old Testament character. He was the one chosen by God to lead Israel out of slavery in Egypt. At Mount Sinai, Moses was the mediator of Torah, the divine law. He was also the law's preeminent teacher. During the wilderness wandering, Moses became the first and greatest of Israel's prophets: one who spoke Yahweh's words to the people, calling them to covenant faithfulness (Deuteronomy 18:15). Finally, Moses was chosen to lead Israel to the promised land. All along the way, Moses was the matchless confidante of God. Moses alone spent forty days and nights communing with God after the idolatry of the golden calf episode (Exod 34:28).

Moses enters the biblical drama at the height of Egypt's murderous oppression of Israel. As a boy, Egyptian scribes probably educated Moses, and his schooling would have lasted around twelve years. Moses' childhood curriculum would have focused on writing, reading, and mathematics. In the early chapters of Exodus, the narrator wants us to get to know Moses' values and commitments. The order of events is significant. We are told that Moses witnesses the exploited labor of the Israelites in Egypt (Exod 2:11). We find hints that Moses is going to intervene in Israel's plight when immediately following are three episodes with Moses fighting against injustice. Moses strikes down an Egyptian who is beating an Israelite slave (2:12). Next, Moses intervenes in a fight between two Israelites (2:13). Then, he defends Jethro's daughter's access to water (2:17). At this point in the story, Moses is a kind of Robin Hood figure who fights for those who are oppressed or unobserved. These episodes signal for us not only Moses' own commitments but also the character and purpose of the law that Moses will soon receive from Sinai and teach to the people.

## Moses' Leadership

The narrator pays a lot of attention to Moses' experiences as a leader. We are privy to the character and trials of this man as he leads God's people. We are invited to reflect on the formation of Moses as a leader, his reluctant rise to leadership, and the successes and (more often) the agony

of his leading Israel through the wilderness. The life of
Moses in Exodus is, in part, a deliberate study in leader-
ship, probably written for the benefit of other leaders in
Israel in later times.

Many of us are leaders of some kind: parents, grand-
parents, teachers, bosses, pastors, and so on. Anyone who
has been a leader knows that being in charge often hurts.
For much of the time, leading is challenging and draining.
Yet, leaders are used by God to mobilize others into kingdom service, and nothing could be more exciting. In what
follows I will focus on two aspects of Moses' leadership.
You might consider reading carefully through the book of
Exodus as a study in kingdom-oriented leadership.

## 1. Moses' Deep Dejection at Early Failures

When Moses and Aaron first declare to Pharaoh Yahweh's
demand to let Israel worship God in the wilderness,
Pharaoh only increases the burden on the Israelites. In
response, the people turn against Moses, saying, "The
LORD look upon you and judge!" (Exod 5:21) Dejected,
Moses turns to the Lord and says,

> O LORD, why have you mistreated this
> people? Why did you ever send me? Since
> I came to Pharaoh to speak in your name,
> he has mistreated this people, and you have
> done nothing at all to deliver your people.
> (Exod 5:22–23)

Moses' first experiences of leadership were very difficult.
Like Moses, many of us have had unrealistic expectations
of some great achievements early in our leadership. Posts

about wildly successful start-ups and the popularity of our own social media posts may fuel our anticipation of early success. Instead of rapid success, Moses is challenged to take a step down and to trust God. He finds that the road to the promised land is strewn with boulders and potholes (for example, Exod 17:8–16). Success in God's terms is different from the wealth-driven, command-oriented rule of Pharaoh. For Pharaoh's kind of leadership has been summarily judged and left behind. "Success" in this book is simply Moses' obedience to God's word and his submission to Yahweh's plans for the people.

Moses is called to what Friedrich Nietzsche has termed the "long obedience in the same direction."[33] This long obedience is seen, for example, in the three thirst episodes. Moses remains faithful as the people dispute with him about water at Marah (Exod 15:22–27). The episode repeats itself at Meribah (Exod 17:1–7), where Moses continues to seek the Lord on behalf of his people. Then, years later, the second generation repeats the grumbling of their parents (Num 20:2–13). You can imagine Moses' exhaustion! In each episode, the people grumble and are ready to run. Moses alone must again muster up courage and energy to call the people back to their task to be a faithful people. When I read these three episodes, I feel Moses' pain. Hasn't every leader been there? I feel like shouting to the Israelites: "Really? You are grumbling *again*? I mean, really? *Again*?"

Moses is not called to kick the season-winning goal every day; Moses is just called to be faithful every day— to say yes to God each new day. In doing so, Moses commits himself again to the "long obedience in the same direction." God was faithful to Moses and to Israel, was God not? So let us be encouraged, fellow leaders, knowing that at each pothole and boulder we encounter the chief Shepherd is nurturing us as his under-shepherds, in order that we may become humbler, wiser, more loving, more mature, and thereby also more useful, under Christ's care.

## 2. *Moses Is* for *His People*

Moses is *for* his people; he is *for* the people of God. Moses' selflessness and his staggering acts of love for the community are key to his leadership. For example, in response to the idolatry of the golden calf, God plans to destroy Israel and to start a new community with Moses and his descendants (Exod 32:11). Moses rejects God's offer for him to be the new patriarch of Israel. Instead, Moses confesses the full gravity of the nation's sin to God. Then he says, "But now, if you will only forgive their sin—but if not, please blot me out of your book that you have written" (Exod 32:31–32). Moses' self-sacrificial love for the people he leads is all the more remarkable in that this episode begins with the fact that Moses ties himself to the future of the nation in this way. He is sold out on God's purposes for the people, and he has thoroughly subordinated his own success and prospects to God's purposes. Remarkable too is that Moses' gracious action follows on what seems to be a popular disparaging remark against Moses: "As for this Moses, the man who brought us up out of the land of Egypt, we do not know what has become of him" (Exod 32:1).

Moses' extravagant acts of love for his people point us to the cross of Christ. For, while Christ's acts of power called forth admiration—"We have never seen anything like this!" the people declared (Mark 2:12)—it was Christ's humility and sacrifice that called forth the deepest loyalty from his early followers. The apostle Paul declares, "May I never boast of anything except the cross of our Lord Jesus Christ" (Gal 6:14). Paul makes himself a student of Christ's humility, reflecting: "He humbled himself and became obedient to the point of death—even death on a cross" (Phil 2:8). Extravagant, sacrificial love is the way of kingdom leadership. We leaders who seek to follow the Lord must earn the loyalty of others not by our greatness but by our self-giving. To be sure, Moses' leadership was full of friction and discouragement. Nonetheless, Moses' profound humility (Num 12:3) and his tying himself to the fate of his people in this way must have endeared many in the community to him with a deep loyalty.

For Christian leaders today, this kind of selflessness and generosity is the narrow way. Let's be honest, we leaders are often just as self-focused as those whom we seek to lead, and our disappointments often breed resentment in us. We can become the accuser of our people before God, rather than their advocate. What would it look like for you to love the people you lead extravagantly? Is God inviting you into an extravagant act of love?

## The Women Who Tricked Pharaoh

Twelve women appear in the opening chapters of Exodus, some of whom by their cunning, boldness, and decisiveness trick Pharaoh and preserve Moses' life in order that God's plans might be fulfilled.[34] Cheryl Exum writes, "Without Moses, there would be no story, but without the initiative of these women, there would be no Moses!"[35] Jopie Siebert-Hommes shows how these twelve women correspond to the twelve tribes of Israel (Exod 1:1; in addition to the women discussed below, the daughters of Jethro make up twelve [2:16]).[36] The exodus of the twelve tribes out of Egypt depends on the resolve of these women who are used by God.

## Shiphrah and Puah (Exodus 1:15–22)

The first characters named in the story of the exodus are not Moses and Pharaoh (the latter is never identified by name), but two Hebrew midwives. These are the first in a "whole array of female characters in Exodus 1–2 who venture to trick Pharaoh as they rescue Moses from the deadly royal decree," as Ilana Pardes puts it.[37] Pharaoh demands that these women kill every male Hebrew newborn. But, as Shiphrah and Puah "feared God," they don't fulfill the request. Shiphrah and Puah take a subtle jab at Pharaoh, implying the superiority of Hebrew women: "The Hebrew women are not like the Egyptian women; for they are vigorous and give birth before the midwife comes to them" (Exod 1:19). This is the first act of civil disobedience for the sake of justice in written history—and God blessed these women for their faithfulness (Exod 1:21).[38]

## Jochebed (Exodus 2:1–9; 6:20)

Jochebed, Moses' mother, tricks Pharaoh by following to the letter his decree that every newborn Hebrew male should be thrown into the Nile. For three months, Jochebed hides the newborn Moses. When hiding Moses becomes too risky, she places Moses in a carefully prepared basket, which she floats in the Nile. Pharaoh's daughter finds the baby, and at Miriam's suggestion Pharaoh's daughter appoints Jochebed as Moses' wet nurse.

Jochebed's name means "Yahweh is glory." This is the first name to appear in the Bible that includes the divine name "Yahweh": *yah*. "Yahweh" is the personal name for God, revealed to Israel. It seems, then, that the name Yahweh was "embedded in [Moses] maternal lineage: if his mother bears YHWH's name, Moses learned it from her."[39]

## Miriam (Exodus 2:1–10; 15)

After Moses' mother places the baby in the basket, Moses' sister stands watch. When Pharaoh's daughter finds Moses, the sister suggests, "Shall I go and get you a nurse from the Hebrew women to nurse the child for you?" (Exod 2:7). The girl fetches Moses' mother, displaying the cunning, boldness, and decisiveness that characterizes many of the women in these opening chapters of Exodus. Pardes refers to these events as "the triumph of the female saviors over the mighty Pharaoh."[40]

While Moses' sister is not named in the early chapters of Exodus, she is most likely Miriam, who is a significant leader within Israel. Miriam leads alongside Moses and Aaron throughout the wilderness years. Miriam's importance as a leader can hardly be overstated. For example, she leads Israel in a song of celebration after crossing the Red Sea (Exod 15:20–21); she is introduced as a prophet (v. 20). Interestingly, Miriam is not referred to as a mother or as a wife, which is different from most of the women in the Bible.[41]

## Pharaoh's Daughter (Exodus 2:5–10)

Another unlikely hero is Pharaoh's unnamed daughter. This woman is motivated by compassion for a Hebrew baby: "He was crying, and she took pity on him" (Exod 2:6). Pharaoh's daughter gives Moses to his mother until the time of weaning (around three years), and then adopts Moses as her own son, "right under her father's nose."[42] Her behavior is rebellious.

Pharaoh's daughter names the baby "Moses,"—"'because,' she said, 'I drew him out of the water'" (Exod 2:10). "Moses" means "draw up/out," also anticipating that, through Moses, God will one day draw up Israel from Egypt and from the Red Sea. The name that Pharaoh's daughter gives the boy frames her as responsible not only for Moses' life, but also for the Israelites' escape.

## Zipporah (Exodus 2:16–22; 4:24–26; 18:1–4)

Zipporah is a heroic figure who saves Moses' life as an adult. Zipporah was one of the seven daughters of Reuel, the priest of Midian (Reuel is later referred to as Jethro, in Exod 18:1). Moses delivered these seven sisters from shepherds when they were seeking to water their flocks. In turn, Zipporah's father offered hospitality to Moses and then gave Zipporah to Moses in marriage (Exod 2:16–22). The firstborn son of Zipporah and Moses was named "Gershom," which means "to drive off/drive out." This name seems to refer to the event at the watering well and to anticipate the exodus from Egypt.

After encountering Yahweh at the burning bush, Moses journeyed to Egypt, along with his family. Along the way, one night, the Lord seeks to kill Moses (Exod 4:24).

Zipporah acts assertively, cutting off her son's foreskin with a flint and touching Moses' feet with it. Her action is skilled and decisive. Zipporah seems to work as a skillful priest, evident by her use of the flint, by her utterance (Exod 4:25), and by her knowledge of the circumcision ritual.[43] Indeed, Zipporah, like Moses, was from a priestly family, and female priestly functions were well known in the ancient Near East. On this night Zipporah was, in effect, modeling for Moses the character traits that he would need to acquire as he confronted Pharaoh and as he led Israel, namely, a deep fear of and trust in Yahweh, and a formidable boldness.

We should probably understand Yahweh's actions against Moses in this event as a jolting reminder to Moses that he should revere the Lord through circumcision. It was the Midianite Zipporah, not Moses, who was attentive to this faithful act.

While God used these women powerfully, God had a purpose not only for individuals but also for the whole nation of Israel. The wilderness was the school in which God's people learned to trust God, as we shall see in the next chapter.

**SUGGESTED READING**

☐ Exodus 2

☐ Exodus 4:18–31

☐ Exodus 6:28–7:13

## Reflection

Does the life of Moses present an invitation for you in your own leadership role?

_____

_____

_____

_____

Is there one characteristic of these women, whom God uses powerfully, that stands out to you?

_____

_____

_____

_____

How does suffering and disappointment shape a leader?

_____

_____

_____

_____

# 6

# LEARNING TRUST IN THE WILDERNESS

*Somewhere is better than anywhere.*

—Flannery O'Connor

## Our Experience of Rootlessness

There is a pervasive and increasing rootlessness in Western cities. In ages past, people found their identity within a particular place. An expression of this is the way the people were recognized and also named in reference to their place—"Augustine of Hippo," for example. Today, many Westerners are thirsty for a place that is theirs, tormented by thirst for a home. In the business sector, it is common for people to switch employers every two years, and a career may play a stabilizing role in our lives that a place used to play. Social media doesn't help, scattering our consciousness toward tens or even hundreds of places every day and leaving us with less energy to put down healthy roots in the neighborhood where our physical bodies subsist. Both the breakdown of intimate relationships and the silo mentality that characterizes urban life can erode our sense of being known in a place. Many of us are wanderers, whether in our minds or in our bodies. The flourishing of urban gardening in many cities, and even the neo-agrarian movement itself, seem to be healthy responses to these currents of displacement. Some of us are "gardening our way home."

In the first five books of the Bible, God's people are in search of a home. Yahweh's foundational revelations—the giving of the law and the lived lessons of Yahweh's provision—are given not during a period of settledness but during a period of wandering. Despite the disorientation that rootlessness incurs—or perhaps by means of this disorientation—wilderness wandering is a place to encounter God. As we read these chapters, we wonder: "Could it be that he is the God who most desires the interactions of the wilderness?"[44] Let's journey with Israel now from Egypt to Sinai and witness how Yahweh is present with us when we experience loneliness and disorientation.

## Trusting God in the Wilderness Watershed (Exodus 15:22–17:16)

Israel journeyed from the Red Sea to Sinai in less than three months, and yet during this short period Israel's life hung by a thread more than once. Israel is invited to trust Yahweh even as they are brought to the edge of life itself.

In the wilderness, between Egypt and Sinai, Israel was invited to trust Yahweh through experiences of great need. Through this experience Israel was learning what it means to be the people of Yahweh—a people who know that at the heart of reality is a generous God. Let's reflect on our own personal experiences of the wilderness.

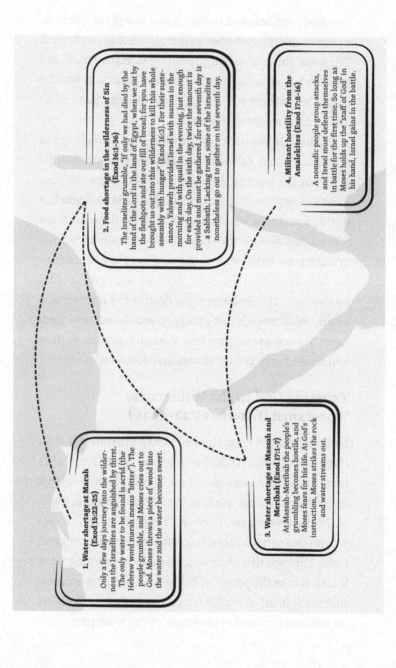

**2. Food shortage in the wilderness of Sin (Exod 16:1-36)**

The Israelites grumble, "If only we had died by the hand of the Lord in the land of Egypt, when we sat by the fleshpots and ate our fill of bread; for you have brought us out into this wilderness to kill this whole assembly with hunger" (Exod 16:3). For their sustenance, Yahweh provides Israel with manna in the morning and with quail in the evening, just enough for each day. On the sixth day, twice the amount is provided and must be gathered, for the seventh day is a Sabbath. Lacking trust, some of the Israelites nonetheless go out to gather on the seventh day.

**4. Militant hostility from the Amalekites (Exod 17:8-16)**

A nomadic people group attacks, and Israel must defend themselves in battle for the first time. So long as Moses holds up the "staff of God" in his hand, Israel gains in the battle.

**1. Water shortage at Marah (Exod 15:22-25)**

Only a few days journey into the wilderness the Israelites are anguished by thirst. The only water to be found is acrid (the Hebrew word marah means "bitter"). The people grumble, and Moses cries out to God. Moses throws a piece of wood into the water and the water becomes sweet.

**3. Water shortage at Massah and Meribah (Exod 17:1-7)**

At Massah-Meribah the people's grumbling becomes hostile, and Moses fears for his life. At God's instruction, Moses strikes the rock and water streams out.

## Wilderness and the Presence of God

In the wilderness, Israel needed to trust God. Manna and quail were provided from day to day, enough—but not more than enough—to sustain them for twenty-four hours. In this way the Israelites were invited to trust Yahweh for every new day. It is the same with God's people through the ages. When our life is "cruising," we have little need to trust in the Lord. I have never heard anyone say, "The year that I really grew to trust God was an easy year!" No, the Lord meets us in the wilderness. For myself, two years lying in bed with chronic fatigue in my late twenties have been among the most formative years of my life. When God stopped me in my tracks, taking away any ability to achieve and succeed, I became humbler and readier to depend upon God. I also learned to slow down and to listen to the suffering of others. Walter Brueggemann reflects on God's presence in the wilderness: "Is wilderness an in between moment without him? Or is wilderness a place which he prefers for his particular presence because of his particular character?"[45] The Lord meets us, especially, in the wilderness.

Nonetheless, it is very difficult to trust that the Lord is attentive to us during these dark periods. It is not a given when we suffer that we will depend upon God. I have noticed that when I am finding it difficult to trust in God, there is also something else going on: I am forgetting to *hope*. Israel grumbled because in the hour of darkness they lost sight of the bigger plans God had for them and for the whole world. Their error was to think that the God of the exodus didn't have any more plans: having emancipated a slave nation, God packed up and went home. However, the exodus was just the beginning. In rescuing Israel, the Lord was writing a new chapter in the world's story, in which not only Israel, but also every nation will be caught up in God's good, restorative purposes for the creation. Christian faith is all about hope. Alissa Wilkinson brings home the importance of hope in a fresh way with this story:

> Last August, in a discussion about virtues, Paula Huston recounted a story that keeps returning to me at the oddest times. She was talking to a monk friend about some struggles she was having with a person in her life who just wasn't doing things the right way, with whom she was getting impatient—nothing big, just big enough to be frustrating to her. "Ah," the monk said. "You need to cultivate hope, then." She told us she'd found this startling—she'd expected to be told she needed to cultivate patience. But hope? Yes: her impatience was an indicator that she had given up hope for change. And what that really meant was she'd given up believing that God would actually do what he'd said he'd do. Which, when you think about it, is a pretty dangerous attitude. One most of us indulge in daily.[46]

During those times when it is difficult to trust in God, a good "way in" is to start with hope. You might reread the exodus story in order to remember again that this is our Father's world; broken and corrupted the world may be, yet it belongs to God. And in Christ, God is recovering the divine purposes for the creation.

## In Pursuit of Land: Invitation to Rootedness

In his magisterial study *The Land: Place as Gift, Promise and Challenge in Biblical Faith*, Brueggemann traces the journey of God's people from wilderness to land and then beyond exile to renewed creation. He observes: "Biblical faith is the pursuit of historical belonging that includes a sense of destiny derived from such belonging."[47] Israel's wanderings were in the pursuit of land and a life of flourishing within that land. Jesus, too, loved particular places. To be sure, as an itinerant prophet Jesus had "no place to lay his head" (Matt 8:20). And yet, Jesus ministered mostly in particular towns around the northern banks of the Sea of Galilee. Amid the towns, terraced agriculture, muddy creeks, and endless hills of Galilee, Jesus walked, prayed, healed, preached, trained, raised the dead, and so on. It is the soil of these hills that clung to his feet and dirtied his hair. The importance of mission in a particular place is also reflected in the letters of the apostle Paul: "To the saints who are in Ephesus," Paul begins his letter (Eph 1:1), or "To the saints in Philippi" (Phil 1:1). We might express the spirit of these phrases like this: "to those beloved of God and called to be Christ's witnesses in this particular place."

The church is called to model the rootedness that God will provide for all God's people in the renewed earth. In a culture that estranges itself from community and place, the church can show what it looks like to love a particular place and to care for particular streets, parks, and people for the long haul. To be sure, some people, like Christ, are called to an itinerant life for the sake of the gospel. Yet, when a local church is invested in the people and structures of its neighborhood, what an impact it can have! While many folks see the church as irrelevant, our commitment to serving a particular place can give us a reputation for community and for kindness, reflecting the love of Jesus. The truth of the gospel must be spoken from a posture of involvement rather than of retreat. Jesus is mirrored to the world not only in speech but also with full-blooded compassion and involvement. Our local church has a beautiful vision statement (crafted before I joined the community):

> Receiving and extending the radical welcome of God in Christ, for the transformation of ourselves and of our neighborhood.

Of course, there are many different ways to extend the radical welcome of God in our neighborhood, but let me zero in on one aspect: reflecting the diversity of the neighborhood. How can we reflect the diversity of the neighborhood in our own worshiping community? In our own church, we try to nurture racial diversity by singing songs in a variety of languages, though the main language of our worship is English. We also strive to reflect the socio-economic diversity of our neighborhood, which is host to both poverty and wealth. We put a high value on sharing meals in our households that reflect this diversity. As for my own family, we have become kindred with a number of people who have struggled with addiction and homelessness. It is our delight to be "family" with our friends, and we are blessed by them in many different ways. Did not Christ eat with all of the "wrong" people, according to the honor-seeking mindset of the first century? Is not this the way of Christ? And is not this way also reflected in the book of Exodus?

In this chapter we have explored how Christ meets us in the wilderness periods of our lives. We have also considered the importance of commitment to and love for a particular place for the mission of our local churches. Yet it is the presence of our God, who is committed to us in good times and bad, that is our life, our source, and our joy. We turn now to reflect upon the presence of God that is represented in and mediated by the tabernacle.

**SUGGESTED READING**

☐ Exodus 16

☐ Psalm 121

☐ Luke 7:36–50

## Reflection

Can you think of a period in your life when you encountered God in a special way through suffering? How did your faith mature at that time?

_____

_____

_____

What are the needs in your neighborhood? In the area where you live, what makes Jesus grieve?

_____

_____

_____

Is there an invitation for your own worshiping community to love your "place"?

_____

_____

_____

_____

# 7

# THE TABERNACLE: GOD'S DWELLING PLACE IN THE MIDST OF THE PEOPLE

Let's fess up: how many of us knew that around one-third of the book of Exodus is taken up with instructions for building the tabernacle and with the description of it being built (Exod 25–31; 35–40)?[48] If we did know this, how many of us have read this text all the way through, detail by detail, curtain by curtain, perfume by perfume, tent pole by tent pole? If only in terms of the sheer space devoted to the tabernacle in this book, the tabernacle is of great importance.

Israel's tabernacle was the place where the Lord dwelled in the midst of the people. So, the word "tabernacle" (in Hebrew, *mishkan*) is related to the verb *skn*, which means "to dwell." The Lord says, "And let them make me a sanctuary, that I may dwell in their midst" (Exod 25:8 ESV). No longer was Yahweh to appear to Israel only occasionally and only on the mountain. Now, Yahweh was in the thick of it all, in the midst of the community, journeying

## TEMPLES AND SACRIFICES IN THE ANCIENT WORLD

Whereas today a church building is a place for us to gather for worship, in the ancient Near East a temple was where the gods were sought and placated. In the temples of Israel's neighbors the gods dwelled through their statue-image that was installed there. The priests fed the gods three meals every day, through sacrifices. If the priests cared for the gods properly, then the gods would bless the kingdom and protect the people, or so it was thought. Israel's God was different. Israel's God didn't need to be fed, though the sacrifices were an important part of human-divine communion. Rather, Yahweh pitched tent right in the middle of the community so that God could graciously guide and bless the people.

with the nation in all of its muck and its mess on the way to the promised land. The main idea is not so much that Yahweh would dwell *within the tabernacle*, but rather that by means of the tabernacle Yahweh would dwell *among the people* (25:8).

The writer of John's Gospel uses temple imagery to explain the significance of the incarnation: "And the Word became flesh and dwelt [tabernacled] among us, and we have seen his glory" (John 1:14 ESV). In Christ, God pitched tent in the middle of human society, joining in its joy, its mess, and its brokenness.

## Why Is the Tabernacle Described Twice?

The first thing we notice in reading the second half of Exodus is that the description of the tabernacle occurs twice. It can be rather tiring to read! As if the enormous amount of detail we first encounter in Exodus 26–31 is not wearisome enough, the author rehearses most of it again in Exodus 35–40! The repetition actually communicates something beautiful. The key to unlocking its meaning is the episode of the golden calf (Exod 32–34) that occurs between the two descriptions of the tabernacle . There are basically three parts to Exodus 26–40. First, in chapters 26–31 God gives detailed instructions for building the tabernacle. Second, while God is still drawing up the plans for Moses, the people build a golden calf and hold a feast in its honor (ch. 32–34). Third, the description of the tabernacle is repeated in chapters 35–40, which detail the actual construction of the tabernacle in fulfillment of the divine command (culminating with God's glory filling the temple). There is an implicit promise in this ordering. Despite Israel's idolatry, God will nonetheless dwell in Israel's midst, protecting them and blessing them as they journey. Following Israel's idolatry, the description of the building of the tabernacle is like a new covenant. In the wake of Israel's idolatry, God gives an extravagant expression of God's presence, the tabernacle—something tangible, visible, and beautiful. This portable building is an assurance of God's covenant commitment to the people—not only to Israel, but also to every worshiping community, at every time. Following the idolatry of the golden calf, God declares that Israel must go to the promised land without the divine presence (Exod 33:5). However, when Moses pleads with God, God relents, revealing the divine nature with these words:

"The LORD, the LORD,
a God merciful and gracious,
slow to anger,
and abounding in steadfast love and
    faithfulness,
keeping steadfast love for the thousandth
    generation,
forgiving iniquity and transgression and sin,
but by no means clearing the guilty,
but visiting the iniquity of the parents
upon the children
and the children's children,
to the third and the fourth generation."
(Exod 34:6–7)

Here is a God who can be trusted with the darkness of our lives. God loves relentlessly, despite our stumbling and beyond rational comprehension. As the world scrapes and tears at us, sometimes the result of our own foolishness, God stays near. And God whispers to us that we are God's own, God's people, God's children. From the darkness, singer-songwriter Leonard Cohen penned these hopeful words:

Having lost my way, I make my way to you.
Having soiled my heart, I lift my heart to you.
Having wasted my days, I bring the heap to you.
...
The walls smeared with filth, I go through a pin-hole of light. ...
And here is the opening in defeat.
And here is the clasp of the will.
And here is the fear of you.
And here is the fastening of mercy.

Blessed are you, in this man's moment.
Blessed are you, whose presence illuminates outrageous evil.
Blessed are you, who brings chains out of darkness.
Blessed are you, who waits in the world.
Blessed are you, whose name is in the world.[49]

## A God Who Journeys with Us in the Muddled Mess

If Sinai's thunder, smoke, and lightning display the unsurpassed power of Yahweh, the tabernacle shows us that this God will descend from the mountain and will journey with Israel in all of their messiness. On the one hand, the image of the mountain calls for great reverence and for obedience to Yahweh's words. On the other hand, the image of the tabernacle invites us to rest, to trust, to know the Lord's presence with us, and to take courage. Both of these aspects of God's character are to be cherished. For it is only in power and majesty that Yahweh is able to confront the might of the ancient Egyptian Empire, to enact a great slave release, and to form a new community where every person can thrive. And yet the wonder of Israel's God is that this God also dwells *within* the community, up close and personal.

The tabernacle is located in the center of the community, and the people are arranged by their tribes foursquare around the mobile sanctuary (Num 2). This beautiful sanctuary displays for the community the presence and the holiness of God. Via regular cultic rhythms, the people encountered God with the eyes, the ears, the hands, and the nose. Yahweh is demonstrating by this a commitment to the journey; Yahweh will go the full distance with Israel (Exod 33:12–17). In the normal course of things, Yahweh will be found not on the mountaintop, but right in the center of things. God is the fulcrum of the community, the hub, the glue, the source, the sustainer, the director who keeps the whole show together. God knows full well that Israel's journey will be full of strife and mistakes. There will be idolatry and power games (Num 16–17), and by their unfaithfulness Israel's entering the promised land will be delayed for a full generation (Deut 1). Yet God has thrown in his lot with this people. God is willing to have the divine name on them (Exod 20:7), staking the divine reputation on them and calling them "my people" (some twenty-five times in this book; for example, Exod 3:7). God will dwell with them through thick and thin, and God can be counted on. For God's own, the thunder and the lightning are set aside, as well as the judgment of the Red Sea. For Israel, it is as if God rolls up his sleeves and says, "Now let's get busy building this community—I will be with you." God comforts Israel—and communities today—with these words: "Be still and know that I am God. I am exalted among the nations, I am exalted in the earth" (Ps 46:10).

## Why So Many Details?

The details in the instructions for the tabernacle and its building (Exod 25–40) seem endless. I'll bet you have not heard many sermons expounding on the ten curtains that surrounded the tabernacle courtyard, their specific dimensions, their loops of blue material, and their fifty gold clasps used to fasten the curtains together. Grip onto your seat and read through (or skim through) this portion of Exodus. As you read, consider: what is the significance of all of these details? Here are three ideas for you to reflect on.

First, the towering theme in these details is that God alone determines how God is to be worshiped. God says, "In accordance with all that I show you concerning the pattern of the tabernacle and of all its furniture, so you shall make it" (Exod 25:9). No instruction could be ignored; careful attention to every facet of the tabernacle was required if Israel's worship was to be acceptable to the Lord. The following description of the building of the tabernacle emphasizes that all of these details were precisely kept (Exod 34–40). God alone determines how the divine will be approached by humankind, for God is the King, the Creator and Sustainer of everything. Those who would worship the One True God enter, as it were, a throne room.

Second, this beautiful sanctuary, constructed so precisely at the Lord's command, leaves very little room for the worship of other gods. As Terence Fretheim says, "There is hardly room for idolatry to make inroads into such a carefully controlled worship environment."[50]

Third, the tabernacle ordered time and physical space through ritual practices that tangibly represented the holiness of Yahweh the God of Israel. In ritualized worship, God's grace and power were mysteriously made real through specific rituals that were performed in sacred space, according to the divine command. For example, an altar of incense stood in the holy place. The high priest offered incense on this small gold-plated altar in the morning and at twilight, at the time when he set the lamps (Exod 30:1–10). The incense to be used on the altar was carefully specified, and this particular mixture of perfumes could never be used for any other purpose (Exod 30:34–38). Probably, the smoke rising from the altar was a symbol of God's presence among the people (see 13:21).[51] These ancient rituals have much to teach us for our present-day context.

In our contemporary age, many cities that were once at least nominally Christian are now thoroughly post-Christian. This shift has taken hold especially in Canada, Europe, and Australia, and increasingly in the US. In Vancouver, British Columbia, where I live, we encounter a variety of traditional religions, and Christianity itself is seen to be complicit with colonialism and ongoing injustice. As a result, for many Christ-followers, the journey with Christ can be filled with doubt. It is difficult for many Christians to believe that Jesus Christ is truly Lord in our pluralistic context. We can find direction for nourishing our faith in Christ, even in our doubts, from the tabernacle texts in Exodus.

Rituals and practices may provide ways to enter into God's story in his world, even when we find it difficult to believe. By "rituals and practices" I am referring to those repeated activities that nourish us to live and dwell within a particular story. As we share in the rituals and the practices that the Lord has given, Christ makes himself known to us. These practices include the Lord's Supper, baptism, prayer, eating together, sharing our possessions, living a shared life together, living in diversity, gathering for worship, practicing justice, seeking justice, and being nourished by the word (see especially Acts 2:42–47). These communal rhythms and practices that Christ has specified for us are key to nourishing our faith in post-Christian contexts. During periods of deep doubt these practices can hold us in faith.

## Creation and Mission

The tabernacle is described in ways that recall the creation of the world. From the perspective of creation, the whole universe is God's dwelling place (Isa 66:1); within Israel, the tabernacle was the dwelling place of God. As with the creation of the world, the tabernacle was constructed in response to God's command. Its particulars are described in a sequence of seven, as with the creation of the world in Genesis 1.[52] Also, the interior of the holy place seems to have been designed as a miniature model of the creation. For example, the blue, purple, and scarlet walls reflected the color of the sky, and the lights on the lamp had the appearance of the stars.[53]

Why is the tabernacle presented as a sandbox model of the whole world? In calling Israel, in redeeming them, and in giving them the law, God is about the work of renewing the creation. According to the biblical narrative, after God created the world humankind rebelled against the Creator (Gen 3). After human rebellion, everything went wrong: sin preyed like a parasite on God's good world. However, God didn't leave the creation and humankind to the destruction of sin's curse. In calling Israel God was, in a sense, starting again—with one particular family. This one people group was blessed and called to live in such a way that showed the rest of humanity what it looked like to be truly human. In Israel, God was starting afresh, for the sake of the world. Israel was an outbreak of the kingdom of God into a world in thrall to evil. This is the significance of the tabernacle being described in terms of the creation of the world: creation is being renewed.

This demonstrates for us something of the identity not only of Israel, but also of the church of Christ. My favorite quote for many years comes from missiologist David J. Bosch, who writes, "The primary mission of the church in the world is to be the new creation."[54] We are to live in such a way that people notice and exclaim, "Oh, *that's* what life is all about! *That's* what God is doing in the world!" The church is to live a life that is transformed by the gospel as a sign to the restoring reign of God in Christ. Through our communal lives of peace, truth, justice, worship, kinship, and prayer, we are showing our neighborhoods what being human is all about. What an invitation!

This is good news; let us not despair! For this is our Father's world. Broken and corrupted it may be, but it belongs to God. And, in Christ, God is busy recovering the divine purposes for the good creation: "For from him and through him and to him are all things. To him be the glory forever. Amen" (Rom 11:36).

The difficult subject of the judgment of God is one aspect of God's character and actions we have not discussed so far. It is a subject that does not sit easily with many of us. We devote the next chapter to investigating the judgment of God in Exodus.

**SUGGESTED READING**

☐ Exodus 26

☐ Exodus 34

☐ Exodus 40:34–38

## Reflection Activity

1. Take a piece of paper. Draw a map of your neighborhood, city, or area. You might draw in highways, roads, and the like.

2. Add in the place where you gather with God's people for worship. Draw in your own place of residence. Add the places of residence of some people with whom you partner with in the work of the gospel.

3. Draw in some of the places where you are encountering your community (workplaces, schools, places of volunteering, places of justice/injustice, and so on).

4. In those places where God's people are living as a sign to the reign of God in Christ, draw a small symbol of a tabernacle.

5. Use your map as a stimulus for prayer.

# 8

# JUDGMENT

We are confronted with the judgment of God in the book of Exodus. God's promise to Moses includes a judgment upon Pharaoh. Moses is to declare to Pharaoh: "But you refused to let [Israel] go; now I will kill your firstborn son" (Exod 4:23). Moses reports God's promise to Aaron and then to the people, who rejoice at the prospect of this judgment upon Pharaoh (Exod 4:21–31). In time, God is faithful to this promise to judge Pharaoh, and a sequence of acts of judgment (the plagues) ensues that culminates in the death of Egypt's firstborn. God also judges Israel for their rebellion in the idolatry of the golden calf (Exod 32:27–28, 33–35).

The celebration that follows God's judgment upon Egypt may disturb us:

> I will sing to the Lord, for God has triumphed gloriously;
>> horse and rider God has thrown into the sea.
> The Lord is my strength and my might,
>> and God has become my salvation;
> this is my God, and I will praise the Lord,
>> my father's God, and I will exalt the Lord.

> The LORD is a warrior;
>
>> the LORD is God's name. (Exod 15:1–3)

Back in the 1980s, when I first learned this as a modern song, we sang it with gusto. However, then and perhaps even more so now, the thought of God's violence or judgment could be a stumbling block to faith for many people.

How is the judgment of God *good news*? Can God's judgment be thought of and spoken of winsomely? How do we answer hard questions about the judgment of God and even the violence of God? Because of the prominence of the theme of the judgment of God in Exodus and because of its harshness to our postmodern ears, we will consider the judgment of God in some detail now.

## Judgment Is God's "Alien Task"

Belief in God's anger, and judgment, is an outrage exclusive to many Westerners. Richard Dawkins, in *The God Delusion*, writes, "Progressive ethicists today find it hard to defend any kind of retributive theory of punishment."[55] It seems natural for those of us who advocate for compassion, justice, and inclusion to feel sympathy for this view. The argument that God, by judging, would be merely adding to the world's exclusion and violence feels compelling.

These hesitations call attention to a vital and neglected biblical theme regarding judgment: judgment *should* disturb us. Judgment should disturb us because judgment disturbs God. In Isaiah 28:21 the prophet refers to judgment as God's "strange work ... God's alien task." Judgment is not God's preferred end for any of humankind. God did not create his image bearers for judgment but for a thriving life within the creation. We must affirm the great love of God for all of humanity. Psalm 36 declares, "Your steadfast love, O Lord, extends to the heavens. ... All people may take refuge in the shadow of your wings" (Ps 36:5, 7). Psalm 36 is speaking of God's protective love for all of humanity. Think too of the well-known passage: "For God so loved the world ..." (John 3:16).

## God's Judgment upon Oppressors

It seems that there is a difference in how God's judgment is perceived from the comfort of Western universities and Western living rooms, on the one hand, and from within cultures that know the harsh reality of conflict and oppression, on the other. From the comfort of the West, any violence feels offensive—especially God's. But in places where violence and oppression touch community, friends, and even family, God's judgment is often seen not only as acceptable, but essential for life to be livable. If Westerners are to understand God's judgment in the Old Testament, it is important to hear from these cultures.

Reading Jose Miranda, a Mexican theologian, was a great help to me in thinking this through. Miranda learned to read the Bible while working with vulnerable workers in Mexico. Living and working with these workers and their families, Miranda yearned for the day when God would establish justice. He writes of the "day of the Lord," that great day that the prophets spoke about when God would return and establish shalom, God's deep peace. Miranda writes that this day "has the sense of 'Finally!' 'At last!' 'This is what all mankind [sic] has been waiting for thousands and thousands of years!' "[56] Immersed in the grief of the world, Miranda longs for this day when oppression is ended and justice is established. It is God's dramatic intervention that will ultimately end oppression. And God's intervention *must* include the judgment of oppressors, for how can shalom prevail when oppressors are still oppressing? We might reflect, then, that the coming of Christ, in salvation and judgment, does not create a problem; rather, it solves a problem—*the* problem—of the mess of the world.

Another help to me was Croatian theologian and philosopher Miroslav Volf. Volf's book *Exclusion and Embrace* asks what a distinctively Christian response to violence and injustice should be. Volf is writing as a Croatian, deliberating on the Yugoslav war of the early 1990s. Highly organized atrocities against Croatians and Bosnians aimed to cleanse the region of whole ethnic groups. It was in this context that the phrase "ethnic cleansing" was first used. In light of such atrocities, Volf explores the relationship between God's patience and God's judgment:

> Should not a loving God be patient and keep luring the perpetrator into goodness? This is exactly what God does: God suffers the evildoers through history as God suffered them on the cross. But how patient should God be? The day of reckoning must come, not because God is too eager to pull the trigger, but because every day of patience in a world of violence means more violence and every postponement of vindication means letting insult accompany injury. "How long will it be before you judge and avenge our

blood," cry out the souls under the altar to
the Sovereign Lord (Revelation 6:10).[57]

God's judgment is in pursuit of the goal of the end of
all suffering. The exclusion of oppressors opens up the
possibility of shalom. God is patient. But endless patience
means endless suffering. In response to the idea that
God's anger and love are incompatible, Volf writes: "In a
scorched land, soaked in the blood on the innocent, [the
idea that God's anger and love are incompatible] will
invariably die."[58]

These cross-cultural insights help us understand and
appreciate the positive view of Yahweh's judgment upon
Pharaoh and his empire in the book of Exodus. Enslaved
Israel yearned for God to come in power and call Pharaoh
to account (Exod 4:21–31). And when God does come in
power, Moses celebrates that "the horse and his rider the
Lord has thrown into the sea" (Exod 15:1). Judgment in the
book of Exodus is good news for slaves and bad news for
people who oppress and kill others in order to gain wealth.

These insights also help us understand why God
descends on Mount Sinai in such fearsome displays of
power, with thunder, lightning, and a trumpet blast (Exod
19:16). As God gives the law at Mount Sinai, these awesome
signs of God's holiness show that Yahweh, the God of gods,
stands behind these laws. Lest anyone in Israel should try
to assume the power and the wealth of Pharaoh, taking
Israel "back to Egypt" (Deut 17:16), they should know that
the King of kings will call them to account.

## Judgment and the Kingdom of God

How does the judgment of God fit into the larger biblical story? Perhaps our journey through the book of Exodus has already shifted the theological playing field for you. Perhaps you have noticed that what the Lord is busy doing in this book is, in the end, for the sake of God's whole creation. In fact, this is true not only of Exodus but of the whole biblical story. The biblical drama is concerned with what God is doing in *history* to restore humanity to the Divine and to one another, *in this world, in real, lived time*—for all time. So here is the new playing field, the biblical one: the biblical drama casts Christ as redeemer of this whole world. The kingdom of God is like a powerful steam train hurtling through history, transporting cargo that is for the healing of the world. All of humanity is called to get on board with what Christ is doing. Or, the kingdom of God is like a colorful, spreading garden that is bringing beauty and fragrancy across the whole world. Following Christ involves living together as a sign to God's restorative reign, even as we wait for Christ to return and to restore all things. As we work and wait, we pray, "Your kingdom come, your will be done on earth" (Matt 6:10).

This relates to judgment in this way: if Christ is to establish God's good purposes for the creation, then Pharaoh can't be king, because Pharaoh mucks it all up. There can be no good news while Pharaoh is still building his store cities by slave labor. Pharaoh, and all of those who would live like him, may be excluded from the good future that God has for the creation.

Of course, we are all Pharaohs, of a sort. To illustrate this, let me share a story. On August 16, 1905, the *Daily*

*News* of London published a letter to the editor by G. K. Chesterton, a Christian writer. Chesterton was responding to an earlier letter from a reader who apparently found religion to be the root of all evil. Chesterton wisely responded: "The answer to the question, 'What is Wrong?' is, or should be, 'I am wrong.' Until a man can give that answer his idealism is only a hobby."[59]

## Conclusion: Can We Speak about the Judgment of God Winsomely?

Let's conclude by returning to the question with which we began this section: How is the judgment of God *good news*? Can judgment be spoken of winsomely? We have seen that God's judgment opens up the possibility of hope for the future. Those who grieve the grief of the world are desperate for glimmers of hope. The world is held hostage by powerful forces, powerful demons, powerful institutions, powerful armies, powerful corporations, powerful consumerism, powerful banks, and powerful individuals (see Eph 6:12). If hope is to be real, we need a powerful God who stands against destructive forces. The judgment of a gracious God is good news because it is grounds for a sure and certain hope, in light of the power of these destructive forces. As we hope, we pray that God would, by grace, save all people.

As we dialogue with our friends about God's judgment, we need to listen very well and speak very sensitively. This is especially so in post-Christian contexts such as my own city of Vancouver. Yet, the judgment of God is surely a part of the good news. How about the good news of a God who stands behind the creation in power? How about a God who weeps with the slave, with the First Nations residential school survivor, with the abused child? How about a God of whom the prophets write: "I have been watching! declares the Lord" (Jer 7:11 NIV)? I pray that we would find both words and courage to express outrage at the things that outrage God, and to express our hope in a God who is powerful enough to secure a future for the world. Let us sing with Hannah, the mother of Samuel:

> There is none holy like the Lord:
>> for there is none besides you;
>> there is no rock like our God. ...
> The bows of the mighty are broken,
>> but the feeble bind on strength.
> Those who were full have hired themselves out
>>> for bread,
>> but those who were hungry have ceased to
>>> hunger. (1 Sam 2:2, 4–5 ESV)

In this chapter we have explored the difficult theme of the judgment of God. However, we are yet to turn our gaze directly to God, inquiring into who God is. You will see in the next chapter that the practice of inquiring who God is (in a book of the Bible) bears rich fruit.

**SUGGESTED READING**

☐ Exodus 7

☐ 1 Samuel 2:1–10

☐ Daniel 5

## Reflection

What is your reaction to God's judgment?

_____

_____

_____

What is *God's* reaction to God's judgment? Do you think God grieves judgment, in any way?

_____

_____

_____

Is there any sense in which the judgment of God can be seen as good news?

_____

_____

_____

# 9

# GOD

## Who is God in the Book of Exodus?

Pause and ponder for a moment: if your understanding of God took very seriously the book of Exodus, what would God be like to you? Who is this God we encounter in Exodus? What if we allow Scripture, specifically this book, to challenge our assumptions about God? (Of course, we need to take the whole of Scripture into account as we do this.)

Before you read this chapter, you might like to take an hour to do an exercise. You will need a Bible, paper, and a pen. Hopefully, you have already read through the book of Exodus. Now, skim through Exodus section by section (see the Introduction for the book's structure) and write down what you learn about God. Do your best to hear the text speak freshly, on its own terms, setting aside for a while your familiar theological categories. Most importantly, be amazed!

## Our Theological Task

In the previous chapters we have been talking about the great acts of God and about God's laws for human community. Now we are turning our gaze to focus directly on God. The implications of all we have seen in the book of Exodus are immense. We have seen the revelation of God in the exodus event. God judged Pharaoh and his oppressive regime and then led Israel to Mount Sinai. At Sinai, God gave laws for a new society in which every person would flourish. Take stock of this for a minute. This is our God! And this God is real! At the heart of reality is our all-powerful, compassionate God. The God who gives you your every breath is also the God who redeems slaves and the God who desires communion with us (Exod 33:7–11). Our God is mighty, unsurpassed in power, wholly just, and good, and our God is busy recovering God's purposes for the creation. God is the king of pharaohs—both ancient pharaohs and today's pharaohs—who commands our reverence and obedience. As we learn about God, we must be swift to obey, ready to play our part in the story. The revelation of God in Exodus also gives us hope: this world belongs to Yahweh.

## A Theology of Exodus

### A New Kind of Rule

We saw in the opening chapters of Exodus that God prefers to work through "the least of these," in the empire's shadow rather than in its glory, silently but observably weaving people into a new narrative about a completely different kind of society and a completely different kind of rule.

## God's Holiness

A perpetually burning shrub displays God's firm command of the creation, this time not in fiery mountains and bloodied rivers, but on a small scale, up close and personal. At the burning bush, Moses experiences the holiness of God (Exod 3:5). We learn in this book that Yahweh has "hostility to anything that offends his holiness."[60] The holiness of God may result in judgment, both against Israel and against other nations. Yahweh's holiness is not only Yahweh's inapproachability—bringing into focus God's might, God's power, God's majesty, God's pre-eminence over all other gods—though it is that (as God commands Moses, "Remove the sandals from your feet, for the place on which you are standing is holy ground" [Exod 3:5]). Yahweh's holiness is also an intolerance of oppression. Injustice is an affront to Yahweh's holiness (3:8). Don't miss this point: God's pursuit of social justice does not appear *alongside* God's holiness in Exodus; it appears *as a part of* God's holiness. Those who oppress vulnerable people will tremble before this holy God.

## The Primary Actor in a Long Drama

God is the primary actor in a story, a drama. God created a good world, with care and delight. However, God's creation was soon corrupted by human rebellion. God set off down a long road of restoring the creation to the joy and flourishing it was intended for.

## Yahweh Knows, Hears, and Sees

Israel's God does not have to be entreated through ritual and magic, as with the other gods of the ancient world.

At the burning bush, Moses learns that Yahweh knows, hears, and sees.

*Yahweh knows:* "I know their sufferings," says Yahweh (Exod 3:7). The Hebrew word "know" has relational and emotional elements, expressing God's intimacy with and concern for the enslaved Israelites.

*Yahweh hears:* "I have heard their cry," Yahweh says to Moses (Exod 3:7). The Hebrew word for "cry" is a technical term for the cry of people who are being oppressed. Yahweh is especially attentive to the cry of poor and exploited people (Exod 22:23; Deut 24:13, 15).

*Yahweh sees:* "I have seen the affliction of my people," says Yahweh (Exod 3:7, author's translation). The sense of this phrase is that Yahweh observes all things as the Great King of kings. God watches, observing injustice, gazing on the edge of a seat like a hawk ready to swoop: "I have been watching! declares the Lord" (Jer 7:11 NIV).

Yahweh's senses are attuned to the world not only in Egypt, but also in Canaan, in Midian, and in every place. God is present, attentive, and powerful, like a loving mother watching her children at play.

## Plagues: God of Gods, God of Creation

The plagues display four aspects of God's character (Exod 7–11):

1. *Yahweh is the Great King*, who is holding Pharaoh to account. For example, in Pharaoh's court, Moses' staff turns to a snake, and this snake swallows up the staff-snakes of Pharaoh's

magicians. This is a sign that the Egyptians will be swallowed in the Red Sea.[61]

2. *Yahweh is the God of justice,* who holds Pharaoh to account specifically for his injustice against vulnerable people. Yahweh meets the long oppression of the Israelites with a long period of plagues upon the Egyptians.[62]

3. *Yahweh is the God of gods,* who has no peer among the other deities. For the Egyptians, the sun was the highest deity. When Yahweh brings about a thick darkness over Egypt, God demonstrates visibly that the sun god is powerless before Yahweh.

4. *The deliverance of Israel is ultimately for the sake of the entire creation.* The combined impression projected in the ten plagues "is that the entire created order is caught up in this struggle."[63]

## The Exodus: A New King and a New Community

Israel is "brought out" of slavery in Egypt so that they may be "brought into" the promised land, and "brought into" a new shared-life of flourishing for all, especially the most vulnerable. The Exodus is all about creating a new community, under a new King.

## Yahweh's Presence Is Known in the Wilderness

Consistent with God's preference to work through the weak things of the world is God's preference for wilderness interactions (Exod 15–17). In the wilderness, the Israelites were challenged to trust in Yahweh for every new day.

## The Law: Yahweh Shapes a Contrast-community by God's Word

Yahweh's characteristic response to human sinfulness is to draw near, to forgive, and with an authoritative word to nourish communities into loving fellowship. This is like a conductor who instructs the orchestra to stop and to correct its performance, in order that the musicians might play together more harmoniously and in order that the beauty of the music might deepen.[64]

## Yahweh is Present with God's People and within the Creation

By means of the tabernacle, Yahweh was in the thick of it all, in the midst of the community, journeying with the nation in all of its muck and its mess (Exod 26–31; 35–40).

## God Forgives Sin

Following the idolatry of the golden calf, which occurred only weeks after Israel's emancipation, Yahweh forgives Israel and pledges to journey with them. Unlike the surrounding deities, Yahweh doesn't respond to incantations and magic, for "I will have mercy on whom I will have mercy" (Exod 33:19). Rather, Yahweh forgives as an expression of Yahweh's goodness. In forgiving, Yahweh is responsive to the prayers and the intentions of people (Exod 33:17; compare 7:4).

# O, Let Us Worship!

This is our God! At the heart of reality is this generous God who sees all, who sides with the poor, who is quick

to forgive, who is busy drawing us together as family, who
seeks the humble, and who is especially present in the
wilderness. This fills us with hope! So we sing:

> No more let sin and sorrows grow
>> nor thorns infest the ground!
> He comes to make His blessings flow
>> far as the curse is found,
>> far as the curse is found,
>> far as, far as the curse is found![65]

**SUGGESTED READING**

☐  Exodus 10:1–20

☐  Exodus 15:1–21

☐  Psalm 148

## Reflection

How does the portrayal of God in Exodus challenge your
understanding of who God is?

_____

_____

_____

_____

In what ways do you see God's character, as it is revealed in Exodus, reflected in the life of Christ?

_____

_____

_____

If your church were to grasp the character of God revealed in Exodus, how could that transform and mature the life and worship of your church?

_____

_____

_____

_____

# 10

# CONCLUSION

I was born in the early 1970s, and even in my short life-time the cities where I have lived have changed and are now thoroughly post-Christian. People's openness to the mosaic of religions and spiritual practices suggests that our culture is also, in a sense, post-secular. This is certainly the case in Vancouver, British Columbia, where I live, write, worship, and teach. To be sure, there are states in the US where the majority of people would identify as Christian; however, the direction of Western culture is clear: while religious belief is more than acceptable, Christianity is often seen as "a part of the problem." Perhaps, this is not such a bad thing. Christianity has so accommodated the idols of our age—idols of consumerism, individualism, nationalism, and even militarization—that it has little authority or even desire to offer an alternative vision for the world. Many compassionate people view the church as an instrument of colonialism and institutional violence. However, this is not a time for despair; rather, this is a time to heed Christ's invitation in Scripture.

The most hopeful sign of the kingdom of God in the West today, in my experience, is that Christ is birthing worshiping communities—many of them small—that are busy loving their neighborhoods and living as a sign to Christ's restoring reign. These communities are not seeking political power, wealth, or influence. On the contrary, they are creatively embracing downward mobilization and living in solidarity with the poor in the name of Christ. These communities are also inclusive, being composed of many ethnicities and economic situations.

We have seen in the book of Exodus that God is busy renewing community, establishing God's loving rule, and restoring humanity as kindred, especially for the sake of people who are marginalized. As biblical history unfolded, Israel did not accept this invitation. And so, because of their idolatry and their practices of injustice Israel was eventually exiled from the land. In the course of time, Jesus as the king of Israel gathered a new community within first-century Israel in order to realize God's plans for ancient Israel through them. The Gospels, too, are all about community. This is why the Lord's Prayer is given in the plural: "*our* Father in heaven," "give *us* our daily bread." There is a sense in which Jesus is forming a community that will operate in the way that Israel was always supposed to have operated. And Jesus' community isn't just any old community; it is a specific type of community. Christ-followers are family, for we share a Father: "our Father."

So, the book of Exodus isn't primarily for individual Christians, because an individual alone cannot display this communal aspect of God's kingship. God, by the Spirit, is nourishing worshiping communities who exist as a foretaste of the kingdom of God by their shared life of worship and kinship. God calls a people in order to create something totally new, for these people together to be outposts of God's loving reign within their neighborhoods and cities. This is so that every human being may participate in the joy and the flourishing of the kingdom of God and in order that every knee would bow and every tongue confess that Jesus Christ is Lord.

A critical part of the Spirit's work to create kingdom communities is our learning to read the Bible afresh. We will experience a new conversion, or many new conversions, as we rediscover God in Scripture. We will praise our generous God, who is at the heart of reality, who gives us our every breath, who is busy lifting up the poor, forgiving sins, and knitting us together as kindred. For Christ is the clue to God's creation: all things have been created through him and for him. "He himself is before all things, and in him all things hold together" (Col 1:16-17). "To him be the glory forever. Amen" (Rom 11:36).

**SUGGESTED READING**

☐ Mark 3:31–35

☐ Acts 2:42–47

☐ Acts 4:32–37

## Reflection

How has reading the book of Exodus shaped your view of
the Old Testament?

_____

_____

_____

How has reading the book of Exodus shaped your imagination for your church?

_____

_____

_____

How is the book of Exodus inviting you or your family to
live as a sign to God's kingdom?

_____

_____

_____

_____

# SUGGESTED READING

Terence E. Fretheim. *Exodus*. Interpretation. Louisville: John Knox, 1991.

> Fretheim's is a brilliant and creative commentary, for thoughtful Bible readers.

Carol Meyers. *Exodus*. The New Cambridge Bible Commentary. Cambridge: Cambridge University Press, 2005.

> Meyer's commentary is for the serious student of the Bible who wants to consider historical issues as well as questions of interpretation. Meyer is a leading scholar on women in the Old Testament.

# NOTES

1. Richard Bauckham, *The Bible and Mission: Christian Witness in a Postmodern World* (Grand Rapids: Baker Academic, 2003), 28.

2. Scriptures quotations are taken from the NRSV translation, unless indicated otherwise. Some changes have been made to the NRSV translation in order to avoid the masculine pronoun for God. On gender for God in the Old Testament, see James Gordon McConville, "Neither male nor female: Poetic imagery and the nature of God in the Old Testament," *JSOT* (2019): 166–81.

3. On the second person singular address, see J. G. McConville, "Singular Address in the Deuteronomic Law and the Politics of Legal Administration," *JSOT* (2002): 19–36.

4. Charles R. Taber, *Graduate Education for World Mission* (Johnson City: Emmanuel School of Religion, 1980), 5–7.

5. Cornelius Plantinga, Jr, *Not the Way It's Supposed to Be: A Breviary of Sin* (Grand Rapids: Eerdmans, 1995), 7.

6. See further "Deuteronomy and Human Rights," in *Theology of Deuteronomy: Collected Essays of Georg Braulik, O.S.B.*, trans. U. Lindblad. N. (Richland Hills, TX: Bibal, 1994), 135.

7. In the ancient Near East, slavery was governed by detailed sets of laws, some of which we still have access to. The Babylonian Law of Hammurabi is the most famous example.

8. Law Code of Gortyn, Col. VI. 46–55. For a translation see, R. F. Willetts, *The Law Code of Gortyn* (Berlin: Walter De Gruyter, 1967), 44.

9. See further Walter Brueggemann, "Pharaoh as Vassal," *Catholic Biblical Quarterly* 57 (1995), 35.

10. Both quotations follow the NRSV, substituting "stranger" for "alien" (or "resident alien").

11. See further Mark R. Glanville, *Adopting the Stranger as Kindred in Deuteronomy* (Atlanta: SBL Press, 2017), 38–39. In

the book of Leviticus, this figure of the stranger may be a person of some means. They may even own Israelite slaves! (Lev 25:47) In the book of Exodus however, the "stranger" is a vulnerable and displaced person. When interpreting the Old Testament, it is important to remember that the same word can mean different things in different books.

12. NRSV, substituting "stranger" and "fatherless" for "resident alien" and "orphan," respectively.

13. Martin Luther, *The Bondage of the Will*, trans. J. I. Packer and O. R. Johnston (Grand Rapids: Baker, 1957), 185.

14. Lesslie Newbigin, *Set Free to Be a Servant: Studies in Paul's Letter to the Galatians* (Madras: The Christian Literature Society, 1969), 2.

15. Christopher J. H. Wright speaks of the "function" and the "objective" of the law as a useful approach for interpretation (*Deuteronomy*, NIBC [Peabody, MA: Hendrickson Publishers, 1996], 13–14).

16. In this analysis, I am following Pamela Barmash, "The Daughter Sold Off for Marriage" (paper presented at the annual meeting of the Society of Biblical Literature, Denver, Colorado, 18 Nov 2018).

17. Both quotations follow the NRSV, substituting "stranger" for "alien" (or "resident alien").

18. Paula S. Hiebert, "'Whence Shall Help Come to Me?': The Biblical Widow," in *Gender and Difference in Ancient Israel*, ed. Peggy L. Day (Minneapolis: Fortress, 1989), 128.

19. Kristine Henriksen Garroway, *Children in the Ancient Near Eastern Household* (Winona Lake, IN: Eisenbrauns, 2014), 108.

20. "Oxfam Says Wealth of Richest 1% Equal to Other 99%," BBC, https://www.bbc.com/news/business-35339475.

21. "Aid in Reverse: How Poor Countries Develop Rich Countries," *The Guardian*, https://www.theguardian.com/global-development-professionals-network/2017/jan/14/aid-in-reverse-how-poor-countries-develop-rich-countries.

22. Moshe Weinfeld, *Deuteronomy 1–11*, Anchor Bible 5 (New Haven: Yale University Press, 1991), 141.

23. For example, Luke 16:19–31.

24. The full story of this class-action lawsuit is told in Mark R. Glanville and Luke J. Glanville, *Kinship with Refugees: A Biblical and Political Theology* (Downers Grove, IL: IVP, 2020).

25. See, for example, John Calvin, *Institutes of the Christian Religion*, 1.8.6.

26. Martin Luther, "Against the Antinomians," in *Christian in Society IV*, ed. Franklin Sherman, vol. 47 of Luther's Works, ed. Franklin Sherman (Philadelphia: Fortress Press. 1971), 112.

27. NRSV, substituting "stranger" for "resident alien."

28. "Our Island is Disappearing but the President Refuses to Act," *The Washington Post*, https://www.washingtonpost.com/news/theworldpost/wp/2018/10/24/kiribati/.

29. See further, Richard B. Hays, *The Moral Vision of the New Testament: Community, Cross, New Creation* (New York: Harper One, 1996), 99–100.

30. "International Trade or Technology? Who is being Left Behind and What to Do About It," CDP Background Paper 45 (2018).

31. A primary focus of the biblical laws more broadly was to restrain the excess and violence of wealthy and powerful people. You can see this goal at work, for example, in Deuteronomy 24:6–22.

32. Craig Blomberg, *Neither Poverty nor Riches: A Biblical Theology of Possessions* (Leicester: Apollos, 1999), 241.

33. Friedrich Nietzsche, *Beyond Good and Evil*, trans. Helen Zimmern (London: T.N. Foulis, 1907), 188.

34. For this section I have been guided in particular by the analysis in Carol Meyers, *Exodus*, The New Cambridge Bible Commentary (Cambridge: Cambridge University Press, 2005).

35. J. Cheryl Exum, "'You Shall Let Every Daughter Live': A Study of Exodus 1:8–2:10," in *A Feminist Companion to Exodus and Deuteronomy*, ed. Athalya Brenner, The Feminist Companion to the Bible 6 (Sheffield: Sheffield Academic, 1994), 52.

36. "But if She Be a Daughter ... She May Live!" in *A Feminist Companion to Exodus and Deuteronomy*, ed. Athalya Brenner, The Feminist Companion to the Bible 6 (Sheffield: Sheffield Academic, 1994), 63–65.

37. Ilana Pardes, "Zipporah and the Struggle for Deliverance," in *Countertraditions in the Bible: A Feminist Account* (Cambridge: Harvard University Press, 1992), 81.

38. David Daube, *Civil Disobedience in Antiquity* (Edinburgh: Edinburgh University Press), 5, 7.

39. Carol Meyers, "Jochebed," in *Women in Scripture: A Dictionary of Named and Unnamed Women in the Bible, the Apocryphal/Deuterocanonical Books, and the New Testament*, ed. Carol Meyers, Toni Craven, and Ross S. Kraemer (Boston: Houghton Mifflin, 2000), 103. The divine name is revealed to Moses at the burning bush (Exod 3:13–14); and yet, in ways not disclosed to us, it seems that God has already revealed this name to the community.

40. Pardes, "Zipporah," 88.

41. Phyllis Trible, "Miriam I," in *Women in Scripture: A Dictionary of Named and Unnamed Women in the Bible, the Apocryphal/Deuterocanonical Books, and the New Testament*, ed. Carol Meyers, Toni Craven, and Ross S. Kraemer (Boston: Houghton Mifflin, 2000), 128.

42. Pardes, "Zipporah," 82.

43. Meyers, *Exodus*, 63.

44. Walter Brueggemann, *The Land: Place as Gift, Promise and Challenge in Biblical Faith*, Overtures to Biblical Theology (Philadelphia: Fortress, 1977), 41.

45. Brueggemann, *The Land*, 41.

46. Alissa Wilkinson, "Advent Hope," Convivium, http://www.cardus.ca/blog/2011/11/advent-hope/.

47. Brueggemann, *Land*, 3.

48. In preparing this section I have benefited especially from Terence E. Fretheim, *Exodus*, Interpretation (Louisville: John Knox, 1991) 263–78.

49. Leonard Cohen, *Book of Mercy* (Toronto: McClelland and Stewart, 1984), 45.

50. Fretheim, *Exodus*, 267

51. Nahum M. Sarna, *Exodus*, (Philadelphia: Jewish Publication Society, 1991), 193.

52. Exodus 25–31 has seven speeches that each begin with "The Lord spoke to Moses."

53. Gregory K. Beale, "Eden, the Temple, and the Church's Mission in the New Creation," *JETS* 48 (2005), 16.

54. David J. Bosch, *Transforming Mission: Paradigm Shifts in Theology of Mission* (Maryknoll, NY: Orbis Books, 1991), 168.

55. Richard Dawkins, *The God Delusion* (Boston: Mariner, 2006), 287.

56. José P. Miranda, *Marx and the Bible: A Critique of the Philosophy of Oppression* (Maryknoll, NY: Orbis Books, 1974), 109.

57. Miroslav Volf, *Exclusion and Embrace: A Theological Exploration of Identity, Otherness, and Reconciliation* (Nashville: Abingdon, 1996), 289.

58. Volf, *Exclusion and Embrace*, 304.

59. This story (and several myths surrounding it) are unpacked in an article on the personal blog of author Jordan M. Poss: "What's wrong, Chesterton," https://www.jordanmposs.com/blog/2019/2/27/whats-wrong-chesterton.

60. J. Alec Motyer, *The Message of Exodus: the Days of Our Pilgrimage*, Bible Speaks Today (Downers Grove, IL: InterVarsity, 2005), 25.

61. Terrance E. Fretheim, "The Plagues as Ecological Signs of Historical Disaster," *JBL* 110 (1991), 388.

62. For more detail see Fretheim, "The Plagues," 394.

63. Fretheim, "The Plagues," 393.

64. See, for example, the second declaration of the Ten Commandments after the sin of the golden calf (Exod 34:1–9).

65. The final stanza of "Joy to the World," by Isaac Watts.

LEXHAM PRESS

# TRANSFORMATIVE WORD SERIES

*An engaging, thematic exploration of the Bible, offering refreshingly unique insights within each book of the Bible.*

*Learn more at LexhamPress.com/Transformative*

Revealing the Heart of
**Prayer**
the Gospel of Luke

CRAIG BARTHOLOMEW

2 CORINTHIANS
CUTTING TIES WITH DARKNESS

JOHN D. BARRY

TOG

THE BOOK OF ESTHER

God Behind the Scenes

WAYNE BARKHUIZEN

When You Want to YELL AT GOD

The Book of Job
Craig Bartholomew

he
SS
ONE
REVELATION

W Y. EMERSON